Supervision of Ministry Students

Regina Coll, C.S.J.

A Liturgical Press Book

THE LITURGICAL PRESS
Collegeville, Minnesota

Cover design by Monica Bokinskie.

6   7   8   9

Library of Congress Cataloging-in-Publication Data

Coll, Regina.
    Supervision of ministry students / Regina Coll.
        p.   cm.
    Includes index.
    ISBN 0-8146-2040-X
    1. Catholic Church—Clergy—Training of.   2. Pastoral theology-
-Catholic Church—Study and teaching.   3. Pastoral psychology—Study
and teaching.   4. Seminary extension.   I. Title.
BX903.C565   1991
207'.1'12—dc20   91-21664
                                                                          CIP

Contents

For Helen,
who taught me so much about life
and compassionate presence to suffering people.

Acknowledgments

I hesitate to name names, having done so in the past, only to realize too late that I have forgotten someone who deserved to be mentioned. On those occasions I have felt like the pastor who, after thanking parishioners for the success of a parish fair realizes that the chairperson's name was omitted. If I do leave out anyone who has helped, please know that I am grateful, if somewhat forgetful.

The students at Notre Dame helped me forge the first outline, suggested topics, and gave direction to the project. Many of them have allowed me to include their contracts, case studies, critical incidents and journal entries. I wish especially to thank John Donato, Carol Guenther, Robert Hannon, Peter Jarrett, Tammy Liddell, William Lies, Thomas MacLennan, Russell McDougall, Michelle Prah, Anthony Szakaly, Anne Volk, and Linda Wall.

In preparing this work I interviewed directors of field education, supervisors and seminarians. As the first draft of each chapter was finished, this same pool of people read the manuscript and offered many helpful suggestions and challenges. I hope they recognize their contributions. For this generous support, I thank Louise Bond, Daniel Durken, Mary Feeley, Jo Giarantte, Patrick Henry, Suzanne Kelly, Bill McCartney, Mary Pat Mulligan. Bob Krieg, Richard McBrien, John Melloh, and Mark Poorman have enabled and supported my ministry. Joanmarie Smith read and reread chapter after chapter, always challenging me to think things through again.

Institutions as well as individuals have helped. I wish to thank the University of Notre Dame for providing me sabbatical time; the Association of Theological Schools for a generous grant and the Institute for Ecumenical and Cultural Research, Collegeville, Minnesota, for creating a place that encourages study, research and reflection and for sharing that place with me.

Preface

In the years I have been working with supervisors of M. Div. Students at the University of Notre Dame, I have been awed by the dedication and professionalism that marks their ministry. They have been models of fidelity and dedication. They have mentored the students and have taught them the skills necessary in the various settings. More significantly, they have enabled the interns to make important spiritual and theological connections with pastoral work.

The question that is repeatedly asked as new supervisors assume the responsibility for educating seminarians and others for ministry is, "Where can I find a book to guide me, beyond the training supplied by each institution?" While there are many excellent books and articles written for Directors of Ministry Programs and for Directors of Field Education, little has been written to help those persons in the parishes, hospitals and agencies who undertake the important work of supervising field ministry. This book is an attempt to begin to answer that need.

Chapter 1 addresses the topic of supervision. In chapters 2 and 3, I situate supervision as education and as ministry. The supervisor is both teacher and minister and as such uses the tools of both professions. Chapter 4, therefore, speaks about learning contracts, journals, case studies and critical incidents. But because ministry is not simply about human service, I have focused on theological reflection in the last chapter. It is the sine-qua-non for ministry and if you are only going to read one chapter, I suggest that this is the one that you choose.

Chapter One

So You Have Agreed to Supervise

You were probably so happy when the seminarian[1] called and asked to come and work with you in your ministry. Think of having another person, even part time, to help answer the needs of the people; think of being able to depend on someone else to conduct a program, preach, teach, visit the sick, counsel. Yes it is a great blessing having a ministry student, eager and enthusiastic, to cooperate with you in your ministry. And yes, they do lighten the load. They will get involved in the parish or in the hospital; they will visit the hospice patients or the prisoners; they will serve in shelters for the homeless and homes for battered women. And, by and large, they will do it well.

But. And this is a big but. The seminarians are not in parishes and hospitals and shelters to facilitate your ministry. They are there to learn. The name of their course, which sends them out from the seminary into the community to learn theology, is "Field Education," and I will repeat over and over, the emphasis is on the noun "education." While the students make wonderful contributions in their field placements, the primary consideration is their education. Agreeing to supervise a seminarian means that you have agreed to be a partner with the seminary or university in preparing these women and men for ministry. On the one hand, they will help with your ministry; on the other, you have undertaken a serious responsibility on their behalf. You have joined the generations of experienced professionals who in one way or another have mentored newcomers to the field.

Professional Preparation

In earlier and more simple times, people who wished to learn a profession would apprentice themselves to experienced and learned mentors. They

---

1. In this work, I will use the words "seminarian" and "ministry student" interchangeably. "Seminarian" is used in most Protestant seminaries for all students, and its use in Catholic settings could serve to assuage tension between seminarians on their way to ordination and seminarians not on that journey either by choice or by law.

learned to heal by watching and working with the local doctor. They learned law or weaving, printing or farming, from experienced lawyers or weavers, printers or farmers. The trick was to choose the right mentor, the one who had wisdom and dedication, skill and educated intuitions.

As life became more complex, as knowledge in the various disciplines exploded, as expectations on professional people became more demanding, the locus of learning shifted to the university. Books and lectures replaced, for the most part, the one-to-one relationship of mentor and apprentice. Even farming and mining became academic programs.

But imagine if you can a doctor who read about medicine but who never served at the bedside of a sick person or a lawyer who read law books and commentaries but who never stepped into a courtroom; imagine a farmer who never tilled the soil, who never harvested a crop. The knowledge of doctors and lawyers and farmers is not only for the sake of knowledge but for the sake of practicing medicine or law or farming. It is important therefore that part of their training involves working in hospitals, in courtrooms, and in the fields.

The same may be said of all professionals who will use their knowledge in practical ways. Teachers, social workers, plumbers, and electricians have some kind of apprenticeship before they are accepted into the profession. They learn from experienced teachers, social workers, plumbers, and electricians the practical skills and techniques they need to carry out their duties. More than that, they may learn from experienced mentors to love and reverence their chosen life's work. They may catch an attitude, as it were, that enables them to forge an identity, to assume the role for which they are training.

For the most part, the training of clerics followed a pattern similar to the one described. As the Church grew, the known world was divided into dioceses with a central church or cathedral. Students for the priesthood lived and studied at cathedral schools, located near the cathedral so that they could apprentice and learn from older clergy. In time, universities were established and flourished, and the training for priesthood was transferred there. There was not a uniform, specified course of studies, and each university provided what the faculty thought best. By the late medieval period the Church was aware of the inadequate preparation of many of the clergy.

In the Catholic tradition, it remained for the Council of Trent to order that training for priesthood be more regularized. In the wake of the Reformation, the Catholic bishops at Trent decided that a seminary should be established in every diocese. This would allow, they thought, not only for the improvement of clergy preparation but also for a greater control over the process. The seminary was to be built near the cathedral so that the seminarians could learn from and be inspired by the bishop and other clergy.

Although writers like Saints Ignatius Loyola and John Fisher had already adopted the expression *seminarium* to describe a place of priestly formation, the Council of Trent gave the first official use to the word. A *seminarium* was a place where seedlings came to life. We might call it a "hothouse" or a "greenhouse" today. The choice of words gives us an idea of the philosophy of education that undergirded the early seminaries. In time, the seminary was moved from the cathedral to more remote areas where there were fewer distractions. Emphasis was on philosophy, theology, and Church discipline. Especially in Catholic seminaries, practical theology was downplayed, but experience has taught the need for more emphasis on experiential learning.

In these post–Vatican II times, seminarians are both male and female; some will present themselves for ordination and others will not. Ministerial preparation is no longer synonymous with presbyterial preparation. Such programs as Channel in Seattle or the Institute for Pastoral Ministry are sending theologically literate and pastorally skilled women and men back into the communities to minister. Clinical Pastoral Education (CPE) has grown dramatically since Rev. William Todd first proposed clinical education for the clergy in 1913. A wide variety of programs are certifying hundreds of students each year. University-sponsored programs in such things as liturgy, pastoral counseling, and religious education abound. In many instances, clergy study along with sisters, brothers, and other layfolk.[2] Protestants and Catholics also join together in these settings. One of the delightful consequences is that a dualistic worldview is being replaced (however slowly) by a more inclusive one. Maleness or femaleness, lay or ordained ministry, Protestant or Catholic, matter less than in the past.

A common thread in these various settings is the requirement that students engage in supervised field education. Styles, settings, and time requirements may differ in each program. Some require a semester or year of full-time ministry; others, part-time ministry concurrent with academic studies. Some require that the field placement be a parish; others allow a variety of settings. But no matter the differences, there is one constant, and that is supervision.

Field-Education Sites

The academic study of the seminary or university is balanced by practical on-site learning in soup kitchens, hospitals, jails, and parishes. "Field edu-

2. Canon law recognizes two divisions within the Church: clergy and lay. There is no pseudo–half step between the two. Sisters and brothers are laity. Reflection on this might erode unnecessary divisions among Christians.

cation'' is a course in which students learn the personal and theological skills of ministry by working with an experienced minister. The heart of the field-education experience is theological reflection shared by the supervisor and student. They do not study theology together; rather, they do theology together. As a result of political and cultural changes as well as the teaching of the theologians of Vatican II, we speak more of doing theology than learning theology, and we acknowledge that theology is not restricted to the reaches of academia.

Some seminaries structure their field-education programs so that the student interns only in a parish setting. They choose this option because that is where most seminarians will spend their lives. It is fitting that the parish be the learning laboratory. The wide variety of responsibilities of a pastor or parish minister as well as the diversity of ages, class, and economic and political variables of the parishioners provide rich and varied experience for reflection. Parish ministers, for example, attend to the sick and dying, they teach (even if only informally), they administer programs, they lead in prayer and worship, they counsel families, they prepare people for the sacraments, they do crises intervention. Seminarians who minister in parishes get the opportunity to work with people, both on a one-to-one basis and also to serve as leaders, especially in the context of worship. The expectations of parishioners vary from parish to parish, but the minister is presumed to be a sort of Jack or Jill of all trades.

Other seminary programs require that students partake in a variety of ministerial settings. At Notre Dame, for instance, the guidelines suggest that a first-year student begin in a non-Church-related setting that involves one-to-one ministry. In the second year, students are encouraged to find placements in Church-related settings, but not in parishes. Third-year students are encouraged to minister in parish settings, where they assume leadership positions.[3] The reasoning behind this guideline is that each setting provides a learning environment that is unique. Particular skills may be more easily learned in a hospital than in a parish and vice versa. Another plus for providing a variety of settings is that students come under the tutelage of social workers, community organizers, campus ministers, prison chaplains, youth ministers, and psychologists, as well as pastors. They may learn some of the skills of each profession even as they become aware of the interdependence of the various ancillary works.

3. This scheme is not written in stone. The age, experience, and interests of students count for much in the choice of settings. For instance, a second-career person preparing for hospital chaplaincy may work at a hospice or a local hospital. We still encourage students, no matter how sure they are of their after-graduation plans, to choose one site that does not fit in with those plans.

The women and men who are interning in the various settings have three goals: to learn the skills needed in particular ministries, to develop a ministerial identity, and to bring their book knowledge into conversation with the lived experience of the Christian community. The community of faith is the locus of theological reflection; it does not merely receive theological insight from beyond itself but generates theological insights from reflection on its experience of God's presence among them. The field placement provides theological content and insight; it is not an arena in which formal theology is applied. It is the arena where formal theology and experiential theology come into conversation. This is an important distinction. Religiously significant information is discovered in the jail, hospital, mission, and parish, even as it is found in a theology text.

For example, one seminarian who is also a member of a religious order learned more about the vow of poverty from what he called "provocative prying" of a poor woman than he could have learned from books or lectures. In his journal, he recorded some of the critical conversation with her. She was an abused woman with three children and an absent husband. Jim, the seminarian, picked her up to drive her to a welfare appointment. "How did you come to have Friday morning off? . . . Oh, a graduate student. . . . I've never visited the campus, I couldn't afford such a school. . . . Oh, you are studying to be a priest, how nice! . . . Do you have a church all set for you when you graduate? . . . No, how will you support yourself then? . . . Oh, a vow of poverty, you don't have to worry about money. That's nice." Her homelessness, poverty, lack of education and security, challenged his ideas about the vows he had taken.

A perceptive supervisor helped him through these reflections but also enabled him to avoid romanticizing the poor by raising the issue of responsibility that each person has for life's decisions. They discussed his feelings of guilt at his own good fortune and the effect that they may have on his ministry. Finally, she led him to understand that he could minister best if he met people where they were now, compromising neither himself nor the persons with whom he ministers.

The Role of the Supervisor

Ministerial supervision is that relationship between an experienced professional minister and a seminarian that aims at enabling the student to grow and function as a minister. We realize that society, parents, friends, spouses, and others supervise one another all the time, but what is spoken of here is formal and deliberate supervision. The supervisor's task is to assist the student in doing and examining present ministry.

The supervisor takes on the responsibility of cooperating with the student in the pursuit of ministerial skills, in the development of a ministerial identity, and in bringing book knowledge into dialogue with the life of the community. Exploring significant issues, inquiring about motivation, probing feelings, clarifying ideas, interpreting behavior, and confronting to facilitate growth are only a few of the ways the supervisor engages the supervisee.

Skills

You can read all you want about riding a bike, driving a car, or playing tennis, but until you start to peddle, turn the key in the ignition, or pick up a racquet, it's all just theory. This is not to demean theory but to illustrate that there are some things we can only learn by doing. That is the basis of field education. Seminary catalogues list such courses as preaching, liturgical celebration, marriage counseling, hospital ministry, religious education, and spiritual direction, and students may read all they want about counseling, consoling, and challenging, but until they can practice in the community, it is all just theory. Field placements become a sort of laboratory in which the ministerial muscles are exercised.

Academic courses usually give some attention to practice of these skills, but a semester is a very short time and the students often do not get enough practice in each course. Immersion in the community provides the time and the place for this practice. This may be a good place to stress once more that the process is called "field education." The noun is "education." The student is primarily a learner even as he or she ministers.

Listening skills may be improved in one setting, teaching in another. It has happened over and over that students learn the place of silence and of appropriate touch in a hospital setting. Sitting quietly, wiping a sick person's brow, holding someone's hand, do not come naturally or easily to some people, especially young people. But after a year ministering in a hospital, students report their growth in "bedside manner and manners." The skills learned and polished in a hospital setting will benefit others in different settings.

While the acquisition of skills is necessary, it is not sufficient. We do not need any more technically correct pastors. Skills cannot be divorced from pastoral and theological reflection. Evelyn and Jim Whitehead[4] caution us that

4. "Educational Models in Field Education," *Practical Theology and Theological Reflection*, ed. Donald E. Beisswenger, Tjaard G. Hommes, and Doran McCarty (Association of Theological Field Education, 1984) 53–54.

learning the skills of another profession (counselor, social worker, community organizer, even preacher or liturgical leader) may result in quite good counseling, liturgy, and so forth, but they may be perceived by the student as nontheological skills. The connections have to be made explicit; the theological implications have to be explored. Such questions as, What does community organizing have to do with one's professed theology? Why are counseling skills theologically significant? We need to talk about skills as skills, but the acquisition of skills must be done in harmony with theological reflection. We speak of the facets of field education under separate categories because of the limits of our language, but each facet affects the others and is in turn affected. The supervisor's job is to make those connections very clear.

While a student may learn some skills just watching and observing a supervisor, mere watching is not enough. I am a student of pottery, a beginning student, a novice, and I have watched my teacher very carefully. My teacher shows me how to turn the wheel, how fast, when to slow it, how to wedge the clay, to center it on the wheel, to coax it into shape. But the actual learning did not begin until I worked with the clay, until I sat at the wheel, until I centered myself as well as the clay. Watching the teacher and the other students gave me some hints, but I had to incarnate the learning, I had to embody it.

I had to try to discover what it means to be a potter, not just to play with clay. What I discovered was that potters are in touch with the four elements of earth, air, fire, and water as they create. They mold the clay from the earth and ever so carefully include just the right amount of water to allow for easy handling. When the clay is ready to be called a bowl or a vase, it is allowed to dry in the air. But even that is a process that needs to be attended to. Too fast drying and the bowl may crack; too much moisture and too slow drying may cause it to lose its shape. Finally, the fire of the kiln hardens the clay, baking the design and the colors in a way that is difficult to predict.

Potters take the basic elements of our world—earth, air, fire, and water—and create something novel, something that did not exist before. But what sets the artist apart from the novice is that the spirit of the potter is also engaged. Molding the clay is an all-absorbing exercise: One's whole body cooperates with the clay and interacts with it. Wedging, molding, shaping, working the wheel—slowly, firmly—the clay responds to the potter and takes form. In the process of keeping the clay centered, the attentive potter may learn to be more centered. More, there is a spiritual relationship set up between the potter and the clay, so that in the process what is hidden in the clay comes to be. The clay becomes something it was not before; in the same way, the potter becomes something she or he was not before. It was no accident that the Lord sent Jeremiah to the potter's house for revelation. The potter's skill was only the beginning of the story, but it was revelatory for Jeremiah.

Ministerial Identity

Psychologists tell us that our identity is formed, in part, by how others treat us. We perceive how others see us and either accept or reject that perception. Even our sexual identity is formed by the way we are dressed, addressed, touched, and challenged, and all this before the age of three.[5] We do not develop an identity or become human in a vacuum. The community contributes to our sense of ourselves. Each of us, of course, processes the perceptions of the community differently. I am not suggesting that our identity is predetermined by others. Rather, it is in the interaction with others that we develop our own identity.

We cannot bestow a ministerial identity upon ourselves, nor do we develop a ministerial identity merely by acquiring certain skills. It is more than doing ministerial things; it is identifying oneself in a particular way as minister. "Minister" becomes part of who we are, not of what we do. We come to recognize ourselves as minister when people allow us to minister to and with them. As they accept our services, when they call on us for help or guidance, when they listen to the word we teach or preach, they help us to define who we are. As other ministers begin to accept us as peers, we further develop a ministerial identity. It is something that is both bestowed and earned.

Supervisors facilitate the process by providing the student with ministerial experiences that stretch them but are not beyond their ability, ones in which they may both experience success and growth. They also facilitate the process by accepting and affirming the student as minister, knowing that they are involved in mystery. What the Whiteheads have written about Christian vocation applies equally well to ministerial identity; the two are inextricably linked. "A Christian vocation is a gradual revelation—of me to myself by God. . . . Thus God reveals us gradually to ourselves. In this vision, a vocation is not some external role visited upon us. It is our own religious identity; it is who we are trying to happen."[6] Ministerial identity is a gradual revelation, not some external role visited upon us; it is who the students are trying to happen. As Christians, we believe that God is present and intimately involved in our lives. Our identity evolves out of that intimate involvement as well as out of the relationships in the community.

---

5. Jean Baker Miller, *Toward a New Psychology of Women* (Boston: Beacon Press, 1976) 70.
6. Evelyn and James Whitehead, *Seasons of Strength, New Visions of Adult Christian Maturing* (Garden City, N.Y.: Doubleday, 1984) 10.

A note from a young woman whom he had counseled did just that for Mike. He was new in the parish and was not yet sure how he was perceived by the community. One young woman asked him to speak with a friend who was having family troubles. The day after the conversation he received the following note: "Dear Mike, Just wanted to drop a line and say thanks for being there for me. I was looking for someone to tell me what to do. I was looking for 'answers.' Although I didn't find any, I feel much better about everything. I seem to have gotten over the frustration, helplessness, and anger (for the most part). I have come to accept it and now it is no longer dominating every waking moment. In fact, it seems so long ago. Thanks so much for being there and for being you!" In reflecting on this in his journal, Mike wrote, "Why was this a critical incident for me? In wrestling with my calling as a minister it has become very important for me to deal with the question of myself as minister. On one level, I had to know whether I would be perceived as a minister; on another, I needed to see myself as minister. I was approached and confided in because of a perception by others of me as a minister. I reacted and knew myself as minister in a way I have not done before." His ministerial identity depends upon his own recognition of himself as minister but also on the acceptance of the community. Of course, one incident does not form an identity; but repeated acceptance and affirmation by the community does.

Integrating Learning

Supervision is one of the bridges (but not the only one) between the world of academic theology and the world of pastoral theology. Making connections is the name of the game. What do the study of Scripture and visiting the sick have to do with each other? What do ethics and Christian education have to say to each other? How do Church history and theories of grace and sin and worship impact one another? How to make professed theology (what we say we believe) and operative theology (what our actions say about what we believe) more congruent?

Supervision is not about discussing issues of classical theology. What it is about is making connections. It is not necessary to be a Scripture scholar or a theologian to ask, Does anything that has happened in the soup kitchen make you think of a Scripture story? How does AIDS ministry relate to how you perceive the Church? Where did you recognize God today? How is grace present in your ministry? What face of sin showed itself? What might Bonhoeffer, Barth, Ruether, Gutierrez, have to say about this situation? As I have already insisted, if supervision were to stop after skills have been developed, it would not deserve the name. Helping the students see connections in their own theology, even though they may not be the supervisor's connections, is integral to the process.

In supervision, Rosa discussed a conversation she had had with a college junior who was worried that her relationship with God was not what it had been. They had shared their views about God and prayer. Rosa soon realized that ideas about how one relates to God affects one's ideas about such things as church attendance and prayer. She and her supervisor were able to connect the conversation with Avery Dulles' five models of Church. They discussed how seeing the Church as institution, sacrament, servant, community, or herald of the word would give rise to different prayer styles and even different relationships with God. The academic theology came alive in the experience of ministry. It was not necessary for Rosa and her supervisor to share the same models of Church or to agree on styles of prayer or on how each might relate to God. What was necessary was a trust and respect for each other that made meaningful conversation possible.

Modes of Supervision

Donald F. Beisswenger suggests seven modes that have become classic ways of speaking of supervision.[7] They are work-evaluation mode, instructor mode, apprentice mode, training mode, resource mode, consultative mode, and spiritual-guide mode. The first four modes place primary responsibility on the supervisor, who may or may not include the student in that responsibility. While much of what Beisswenger describes is valuable, I believe that these processes maintain the student in a subordinate and dependent position and that they are adequate only in the very beginning of a first field experience.

The goal of the work evaluation mode is the accomplishment of the tasks assigned. The supervisor defines the work and evaluates the performance. As I see it, this matter is better addressed outside of supervision. Task assignments and holding the student accountable are necessary, but they are better taken care of before the supervisory session at staff meetings or planning sessions. I would be concerned about a seminarian who needed a good deal of this low-level attention.

The instructor mode keeps the responsibility on the supervisor, maintaining the relationship in the professor-student model. Emphasis is on the cog-

7. "Differentiating Modes of Supervision in Theological Field Education, *Theological Field Education: A Collection of Key Resources* Vol 1, ed. Donald F. Beisswenger, Tjaard A. Hommes, and Doran McCarty (Association for Theological Field Education, 1977) 29–37.

nitive and logical and whether the student is learning what the supervisor thinks should be learned. Certainly the supervisor has much to contribute to describing and establishing an educational climate, setting goals, and maintaining norms, but the education belongs to the student. I don't think we should continue educational processes that promote dependency. In the case of dependent students, every effort needs to be made to help them come to a position of responsibility for their own education. Ministry is not for the dependent.

In the apprentice mode the student shares the responsibilities of the supervisor, learning through observing and working with the supervisor. There is some attention paid to the goals the ministry students set for themselves, but learning is almost by osmosis. This mode still depends more upon the supervisor than the seminarian. The danger is that seminarians may think that the modeled behavior is the only way or the best way to handle a situation. Worse, they may try to be clones of an admired supervisor.

The fourth mode is the training mode, where the professional and personal growth is defined by supervisor and supervisee together. The student is socialized into a clearly defined role in a particular setting where certain skills are expected of all professionals in that specialized setting. It is a mode that has been used in formal training sessions in hospitals, hospices, jails, shelters for the homeless, and battered women shelters. While ministerial skills are transferable from one setting to another, certain attitudes and behaviors are appropriate in a hospital, for instance, that may not be appropriate in a shelter for battered women and vice versa. The training mode socializes a student into specialized ministries.

I hope it is clear by now why I believe that each of the previous modes may be more appropriate only in the beginning of a supervisory relationship. The two modes most valuable for students over the long haul are the resource mode and consultative mode. In both, the primary responsibility is on the student, and the process is collaborative. In the resource mode the supervisor assists the student in reflecting on ministry and in exploring what resources are available. Ministerial situations are examined to discover ways of approaching the issue and what resources may be helpful: What is available in the community? What are the Churches doing? Who is the person who can get things done? How does the parish council operate? Who can be called on? Where can referrals be made? In other words, the resource mode gives the seminarian access to the means to get the assigned job done.

The consultative mode is collaborative but the student takes the initiative. The student is responsible for raising issues and concerns and for coming to his or her own solution to problems and questions. The supervisor's role is to assist the student to develop the capacity to act maturely in solving future problems. This may sound as if the seminarian does the most difficult work here, but the reality of the situation is just the opposite. The supervisor is not a passive participant but is actively involved, alert to verbal and non-verbal clues, giving full attention to the student and the student's issues. Consultation requires a perceptive supervisor who is able to suggest alternatives, to call attention to the consequences of decisions, to firmly and gently confront, and to challenge, challenge, challenge. The purpose of challenge and confrontation is to facilitate insight on the part of the student. It is always done in a positive manner.

Theological reflection is at the heart of ministerial supervision. The spiritual guide mode, in which both supervisor and seminarian seek to understand God's presence in the ministry at hand, is a mode of supervision that complements and completes both resource and consultative modes. The language of "spiritual guide" makes me nervous, however, and I caution that the supervisor is not a spiritual director. The matter for supervision is ministry, not the student's spiritual life.

Supervisor–Supervisee Differences

The supervisor and student enter into a kind of partnership, but a partnership that recognizes differences. There are three major areas of realistic differences between supervisees and supervisors: "First, there are differences in knowledge, skills and experience. . . . Second, there are differences in goals, interests and theoretical orientations. . . . Third, there are differences between the religious personal belief systems."[8] The first and second areas of differences are somewhat obvious and have already been remarked. The supervisor is more experienced and knowledgeable in the ministerial setting. The supervisor has different goals in the setting—they may be the healing of broken persons, systemic change, counseling, teaching, or administrating. The student's goal is learning. The setting itself is not the primary focus of interest. Most students and supervisors have little trouble recognizing and adjusting to these differences.

But in taking the third set of differences seriously, supervision, according to Edwin Hoover, may move from poor to adequate to excellent. Poor supervision rejects differences as unimportant and unacceptable and therefore never enters into honest exchange. Adequate supervision tries to ignore the differ-

8. Edwin A. Hoover, "The Distinctions Between Adequate and Excellent Supervision: A Wholistic Perspective," *Pastoral Theology and Ministry,* ed. Donald F. Beisswenger and Doran McCarty (Association for Theological Field Education, 1983) 224.

ences and pretend that they do not affect ministry. Supervision that is only adequate holds a sort of live-and-let-live attitude, acting as if all ideas, principles, convictions, are equally valid; as if it is only necessary to articulate our beliefs, never to have them challenged but only affirmed. Hoover maintains that the difference between adequate and excellent supervision lies in a situation in which "differences are used regularly to enhance and enrich the learning experience for both the supervisee and supervisor."[9]

Personal religious belief-systems include a person's beliefs about the world, humankind, and God and are based on experience, myths, and hopes. They also include the person's belief about how he or she fits into the picture. Personal belief systems lead to behaviors that indicate one's operative theology, as distinguished from professed theology. Sometimes what we profess to be our theological stance is at variance with the way we actually relate to God, to others, and to ourselves.

Perhaps two of the best indications of our operative theology are our checkbook and our appointment book. Where do we spend our money, to which causes do we contribute, do we spend more than we earn, do we save anxiously for our own future? How do we spend our days, is every minute filled with no time for prayer, rest, reflection? What issues demand a commitment from us? How do we balance work and play? A measure of what is important to me is what I have time and money for. Our checkbook and appointment book say a great deal about the God we believe in, about what we think human life is really about. The answers we give to such questions tell us a great deal about our relationship with God, others, and ourselves. As I reread these questions, I am all too aware that I am speaking for the most part to middle-class people, parishes, and institutions. The poor cannot use the measure of the checkbook or appointment book; being poor is a full-time job.

What Supervision is Not

Often when there is a problem in supervision it is because there has been a confusion of roles. We directors of field-education programs are often not clear enough about what is expected of supervisors. We are even less clear about what is not expected of supervisors. We don't set out the boundaries firmly enough. We are too fuzzy about expectations.

We can learn a great deal by way of negatives. A popular children's game has all the participants keep a secret from one person, who has to ask a question that demands a yes or no answer. If the answer to Is it . . . ? Is it . . . ?

9. Ibid., 225.

Is it . . . ? is a series of no's, a perceptive questioner can often guess the mystery topic. In theology we speak of *via negativa* as one way of discovering what God is like. God is not . . . , God is not . . . , God is not . . . , finally leads us to surmise what God may be.

Before we look at some of the relationships that may get in the way of supervision, let me say that supervision is involved in every one of the following topics. What I am calling for here is a balance, a focus that keeps the main purpose of the relationship in perspective. When I say, "Supervision is not . . . ," there is another part of me that is saying, "Oh, yes it is." Overseer, friend, therapist, and spiritual director all add a significant dimension to the process of supervision. They do not define the supervisory relationship, but neither are they entirely out of the realm of supervision.

The Supervisor Is Not an Overseer

A television commercial shows Inspector Twelve pulling, tearing, stretching, and otherwise doing battle with underwear. Finally satisfied, she stops and says, "It ain't Hanes till I say it is." Inspector Twelve is not an overseer, checking on every little aspect of the work, and in this respect she may be a model for ministerial supervision. She doesn't stand over the workers to see that the job is done, she doesn't check on each step of the process, she doesn't interfere with every facet of the work. She expects that the job will be done and that the final product will be good enough to stand some hard testing. So it is with supervision. We begin with the expectation that the assigned work will be done. Seminarians are expected to be mature adults, not children who may need careful watching over. They may be learning how to minister better, but they do not need someone peering over their shoulders at every turn. Supervision for ministry demands a high degree of trust. If it should happen that assigned work is not carried out and carried out well, that is an issue that may be taken care of as it occurs, but it ought not be the essence of the supervisory sessions.

One important difference between Inspector Twelve and supervisors is that the supervisor cannot say, "It ain't ministry till I say it is." That pronouncement is one that belongs to a higher authority.

The Supervisor Is Not a Best Friend

Supervision may be, and at its best is, a friendly relationship. But the purpose of the relationship is not to become buddies. Friendship demands a commitment that may get in the way of supervision, even as supervision demands a commitment that may get in the way of friendship. Confusion between the two brings with it an overlay of feeling and emotion that can blind both supervisor and supervisee to significant issues in ministry.

If the people involved happen to be or to become friends, a concerted effort is necessary to leave friendship at the door when the supervisory sessions are in place. Just as we do not expect husbands and wives who work together to intrude their marital and family concerns into the professional relationship, so friends may do well to make a pact that during supervision, positive or negative feelings that accompany the friendship will be kept at bay. If you have ever tried to keep such feelings at bay, you know how easily they can sneak in the back door.

It is probably better to imitate the medical profession and set the standard that a doctor does not take care of his or her own family. The demands of spousal or parental relationships and the demands of a doctor-patient relationship are enough in conflict that most doctors keep them separated. At the same time, let me repeat that the supervisory relationship is best carried out when it is a friendly one. The point is that supervision is a relationship whose purpose is to focus on the student; friendship does not tolerate such one-sided attention.

The Supervisor Is Not a Therapist

Recent surveys indicate that doctors, lawyers, and other professionals have good grades in referring matters to someone else if they are not sure how to handle situations. We speak easily about second opinions in medical matters or consultations among law colleagues. Unfortunately, clergy do not get such high marks on referring difficult matters to others who may be better qualified. It is partly because we try to be all things to all people and partly because all people want us to be all things to them. People are not used to hearing a pastor say, "I don't think I am the best one to help you with this."

And so, when a student may need professional counseling or therapy, some well-meaning supervisors attempt to play pop psychologist. Supervision is not the place where personality problems are solved. They may show themselves readily in the relationship, but they are not meant to be the matter of supervision. The matter of the supervisory relationship is ministry. Just as supervision is not friendship but may be friendly, so too, supervision is not therapy but may be therapeutic.

The Supervisor Is Not a Spiritual Director

While recognizing the significance of theological reflection (see Appendix, on priestly formation), it is also important to recognize that the supervisor does not take the place of the spiritual director. Supervision of necessity involves the student's relationship with self, others, and God. But the meat of the process is the ministerial experience. The supervisor and the student are in a relationship that arises out of a concern for ministry. It is the ministerial situation and the student as minister that are the center of the reflection shared. The inner life of the seminarian is best left in the hands of a trained spiritual guide or companion.

Patron Saints for Supervisors

We humans need symbols and myths and models as much as we need food and drink. They are the nourishment for our souls. It is for this reason that the Church has held up patron saints through the ages. Their lives and deaths become the myths, the symbols by which we may better understand our own.

I offer here for your consideration two patron saints but only one model for supervisors—two who are often forgotten in the shadow of their students. I speak of Priscilla and Aquila, wife and husband, tentmakers, fellow workers of Paul, teachers of the learned Apollos, leaders of the Christian community that met in their home, ministerial supervisors. We may infer that they supervised Paul in his pursuit of a trade. "Paul approached them and because he was of the same trade, he made his home with them and they carried on business together; they were tentmakers" (Acts 18:18). Now we know that Paul was busy, like Martha, about many things, and we may guess that as a result he was a bit rusty in the making of tents. He also could not have carted the tools and resources necessary for tentmaking around with him. So he came and lived and worked with Priscilla and Aquila. Perhaps they showed him some new fabric just in from Thyatira bought from a neighbor of Lydia, the seller of purple fabric. Or they helped him to hone his skills, to polish the tools of the trade. The point is that they were the full-time tentmakers and had something to teach him.

Supervisors are more experienced than seminarians and have freer access to the tools of the trade. It is not that seminarians are devoid of skill and learning, but their skills need to be polished, they need to get a better feel for the fabric of ministry, they need to learn how and when to cut so that the strength of the material is preserved, they need to learn to sew that the pieces of fabric fit together and form a sturdy shelter for those to whom they minister.

But sharing skills and resources was not the only thing Aquila and Priscilla were about. They took on another student who had other needs. "Now there arrived at Ephesus a Jew named Apollos, an Alexandrian by birth, an eloquent man, powerful in his use of Scriptures. He had been instructed in the way of the Lord and was full of spiritual fervor; and in his discourses he taught accurately the facts about Jesus, though he only knew John's baptism. He now began to speak boldly in the synagogue where Priscilla and Aquila heard him; they took him in hand and expounded the new way to him in greater detail" (Acts 18:24-26).

If their work with Paul was in the area of skills, their work with Apollos was theological reflection. They may have found themselves, as do some supervisors, intimidated by the expertise and learning of their student. They listened to Apollos in the synagogue, they learned from him. But they had insights into the good news that the eloquent Apollos needed to hear. His accuracy concerning the "facts about Jesus" was not enough. So "they took him in hand." What a marvelous way of saying that they trusted their own authority and experience.

The supervision of Priscilla and Aquila touched not just their two illustrious students but the whole Church. We know how much Paul influenced the face of Christianity but have only a few hints about the contributions of Apollos. Perhaps the most significant is that when Paul warned the Corinthians not to boast or be in conflict about who it was who led them to Jesus, he mentioned Peter and Apollos and Paul in the same breath (Acts 3:4, 22).

It is not just that they shared skills and theological reflection; Priscilla and Aquila knew when their job was finished. Although they wanted Paul to stay and may even have been tempted to go with him, they only shared part of his journey. "Paul set sail for Syria accompanied by Priscilla and Aquila. At Ephesus he parted from them and went himself into the synagogue where he held a discussion with the Jews" (Acts 18:18).

Good supervisors know when students should "go themselves into the synagogue." They do not set up a dependency relationship with seminarians. They do not maintain the student in a dependent position but provide opportunities for growth and independent behavior. Nor do they themselves become so dependent on the relationship that they find it difficult to let go of the seminarians.

Twice Paul sent greetings to the congregation at the home of Priscilla and Aquila. When he wrote to the Church at Corinth and to the Romans he mentioned them by name and then located them within the Christian community. Priscilla and Aquilla were no free-lancers but firmly rooted within the Church.

Conclusion

Perhaps my remarks on supervision make it sound like an impossible task. It is, just as the ministry that you are engaged in is an impossible task. What sustains us is the conviction that we are not alone. Ministerial supervision is not a relationship between two people. It is a relationship between supervisor, supervisee, and the God who loves both. It is a work that touches on mystery. It is "essentially a shared exploration in which the participants arrive at a place which, individually, they would not find."[10]

There is no simple answer to the question of how best to supervise, but a while back I came upon ten commandments for educators,[11] which I have adapted for supervisors:

Ten Commandments for Supervisors

1. You shall not try to make the seminarians into your own image and likeness; one is enough.

2. You shall not refuse a student's need, or refuse your consideration, solely because of the trouble he or she causes.

3. You shall not blame heredity or the environment in general; people can surmount their environment.

4. You shall never give a seminarian up as hopeless.

5. You shall try to help ministers-in-the-making become, on the one hand, sensitive and compassionate and, on the other, tough minded.

6. You shall not steal from the seminarians their rightful responsibility for determining their own conduct and accepting the consequences thereof.

7. You shall honor the students engaged in the pursuit of learning and share with them the discipline of knowledge and skills with which you are familiar.

8. You shall have no universal remedies or expect miracles.

9. You shall cherish a sense of humor, which may save you and the supervisee from becoming either depressed or complacent.

10. You shall remember the sacredness and dignity of your calling, and, at the same time, you shall not take yourself too seriously.

10. Barry K. Estadt, O.F.M.Cap., "The Core Process of Supervision," *The Art of Clinical Supervision,* ed. Barry Estadt, John Compton, and Melvin C. Blanchette (New York: Paulist, 1987) 15.

11. J. R. Kidd, *How Adults Learn* (New York: Association Press, 1973) 306–307.

Points for Reflection

1. Imagine you are responsible for choosing field sites for ministry students. Where would you choose? Why?

2. What are the skills a seminarian could learn at your ministerial setting?

3. How do you share your uncertainties concerning your faith without adding to the confusion of the student?

4. How would you handle a situation in which a student avoided work, was habitually late or absent, or did not perform tasks assigned?

5. What models of supervision as described by Beisswenger are you comfortable with? What models would you construct for supervision?

6. How may friendship enhance a supervisory relationship? How may it get in the way?

7. What is the best thing you, as a person, have to offer a ministry student? As a minister? What are your limitations as a supervisor?

8. How do you deal with conflict? How do you model those skills in your supervision?

9. How has success or failure prepared you as a minister? As a supervisor?

Chapter Two

Supervision as Ministry

Is supervising a seminarian going to be a distraction to your work? Will it get in the way of the really important ministry that you have to do? More to the point, does supervision itself have anything to do with ministry? Does it fit into your idea of what it means to be a Christian minister? Undertaking this new role may be a good time to take stock of your ideas about ministry. In this chapter, I will share some of my views on the subject and make a case for including supervision under the rubric of ministry.

Some people speak of the ministry of priests and ministers as "Ministry" and the ministry of other Christians as "ministry." We know how important our choice of words is, but this reminds us just how important even upper and lower case can be. Capital *M* Ministry is that ministry usually associated with ordination. Lower case *m* ministry is the ministry that flows from baptism and confirmation and for which every Christian is responsible. It seems to me that common practice has it backwards. If baptism and confirmation are the sacraments of ministry for all Christians and ordination is the sacrament of ministry for some Christians, then the major category is "Christian Ministry" and the subset is "ordained ministry."

Some might see this as an attempt to put down ordained ministry. But if we examine the language of that last sentence, we can see just how necessary it is to change common practice. If we perceive ordained ministry as better than, higher than, more sanctified than other ministries, then any comparison of the ministries of ordained and nonordained persons appears to be a "put down" of the clergy. But if we understand ordained ministry as an important ministry among others, the M-m distinction ought to be reversed.

This simple change in the use of upper and lower case would have an effect on our theology. It could go far in helping Christians take their baptismal right and responsibility for ministry more seriously. It may help all of us to recognize what is and what is not ministry. The question of how the work of the Church is to be shared, that is, how ministries are to be shared, is as old as the Church itself.

How Ministry Has Changed

Our earliest Church documents tell us that as new needs arose, the Church responded by creating new ministries. The Acts of the Apostles record that when the Greek Christians complained because the widows among their number were neglected in the daily distribution, the Twelve called the community together and said, "It is not right that we should give up preaching the word of God to serve tables." They then advised the disciples to choose seven of their number to serve at table so that they themselves might be free to pray and devote themselves to the ministry of the word. When the community agreed, they chose seven men, and the apostles prayed over them and laid hands on them (Acts 6:1-6).

Elisabeth Schüssler Fiorenza calls our attention to the fact that the reason the seven were chosen was to free the apostles for ministry of the word. The seven were table ministers. Yet, even though Luke seems to resolve the conflict by a clear-cut assignment of ministries (the *diakonia* of the word and the *diakonia* of the tables), subsequent stories in Acts indicate that the seven preached, became missionaries, and were expelled from Jerusalem after the martyrdom of Stephen. So, even in our earliest days we had not only a variety of ministries but also an overlapping of ministries.[1]

We have in this text a good model for the establishment of new ministries: There was a need that could not be met by the existing ministers. The need was brought to the attention of the Church leaders, who called together the community to address the question. The newly elected ministers not only came from the community but were elected by the community, who presented them to the apostles to pray over them and lay hands on them.

Edward Schillebeckx reminds us of this interdependence of the community and the community leaders in the selection of ministers. "The call by the community is the specific ecclesial form of the call by Christ. Ministry from below is ministry from above."[2] The Church does not appoint leaders the way General Motors or IBM does. Christian leaders exist for the benefit

---

1. The seven are sometimes referred to as deacons, but that appears to be anachronistic: They may have been the forerunners of deacons. Whatever their title, it is interesting to note that the ministry of the apostles was the preaching of the word. Serving the meal was the province of the seven.

2. *Ministry: Leadership in the Community of Jesus Christ* (New York: Crossroad, 1981) 68.

of the community, not for the enhancement of the institution. The laying on of hands "is the liturgical and sacramental expression of the sense of the community that what happens in the *ecclesia* is a gift of God's Spirit and not an expression of the autonomy of the church."[3] The difficulty the Greek disciples had with the Hebrews provides insight into those elements necessary for the establishment of new ministries: unmet needs, involvement of the community, and confirmation by the leaders of the Church. Since apostolic times, these elements have shown themselves to a greater or lesser degree and in a variety of ways when alternative ministries have been called for.

Through the ages, ministries flourished or died in response to the needs of each day. In the Middle Ages, an order of monks was founded to minister by building bridges. Some sisters ran jails and inns. When the number of orphans exceed the number of families able and willing to care for them, orphanages were built. When society later realized that orphanages were not the best place to nourish and foster growth among children, the number of orphanages decreased. Ministry to AIDS patients, to the homeless, to undocumented aliens, are among the most obvious responses to the poorly met needs of our own day.

It is no secret that there has also been an explosion of Church-related ministries. We have even had to develop a new vocabulary to describe the phenomenon. Lectors, pastoral associates, liturgy coordinators, music ministers, Eucharistic ministers—terms we have become so familiar with—were unknown to our grandparents. But there is one Church-related work that is not often described in terms of ministry, and that is the ministry of supervising seminary students as they work within the community. Before we try to understand supervision as ministry, it may be well for us to explore what is being said about ministry today.

Toward a Definition of Ministry

It may not be as easy as it sounds to agree on a definition of what ministry is. Take a moment to decide what you would include in such a definition. How broad or how narrow do you think the word should be? What is included? What excluded? Just as we hold to various models of Church, so we also have various definitions of ministry.

Any society in the midst of profound change finds it difficult to agree on definitions. Our society is no exception. The trouble we have in agreeing on a definition of the term "ministry" is similar to the trouble educators have had in defining the term "education." Too often education was thought

3. *Ibid.* 68.

to be the province of schools and universities. The contributions of libraries, newspapers, concert halls, apprenticeships, electronic media, were not included.

Once we agree that education is not synonymous with schooling, the word "education" can expand to include almost any experience. We do, after all, learn when we fall on our face, either literally or figuratively. But falling on our face does not come under the rubric of education. If everything is education, then nothing is education. If everything is education, then we have no agreed-upon vocabulary with which to discuss the topic; we are unable to set criteria for good education, to measure advances, or plan for subsequent educational experiences. Good education requires a degree of conscious, deliberate practice on the part of the educator.

In a similar way, when we speak of "ministry" we sometimes stretch the term so that every good deed is subsumed under the rubric of ministry. All good works, Christian charity, and even polite courtesies are raised to the level of ministry. And perhaps the crux of the matter lies in the use of the word "raised." If we perceive ministry to be somehow better than or higher than other good works, then in order to enhance these good works we resort to calling them ministry. It may be that our exaltation of ministry is an indication that hierarchical thinking is not a thing of the past. It would help in the rest of this discussion if we could remember that "the gifts we possess differ as they are allotted to us by God's grace, and must be exercised accordingly" (Rom 12:6). Suggesting that there are many good works that are not ministry is not to degrade them. Ministry is not in itself better than Christian service or Christian charity. Or for that matter, Jewish or Islamic service or charity.

But ministry can also be defined in such a narrow way that only the service of ordained ministers or laity commissioned by the institutional Church is included. In this model, ordination to the priesthood or the commissioning of lay ministers by a pastor or bishop is a necessary prerequisite for ministry. This definition restricts ministry to mean the kinds of things associated with the clergy: preaching, presiding at liturgy, administering the church community.

In the years before Vatican II it was easier for Catholics to define ministry because it was popularly acknowledged to be the province of the clergy. The clergy had a ministry, sisters and brothers had an apostolate, and the laity were the people they did it to. Even the index of *The Documents of Vatican II*[4] lists "see clergy" under the heading "Ministry." Just a few years ago,

4. Walter M. Abbott, S.J., *The Documents of Vatican II* (New York: America Press, 1966).

the administrative board of the National Council of Catholic Bishops announced that when it used the word "ministry" it would refer to activities of the ordained or those commissioned by the Church. Other works would be called "Christian service." The theologians among the bishops replied, however, that it would be premature to try to close off the meaning of the word. We are still in the process of defining what the word will mean for us.

But in that process we do not make meaning out of whole cloth; we rely on the sense of the community to assist us in our search. A quick look at what others have said about ministry can help us to realize just how complex the problem is, and, at the same time, it can clarify some of our questions. The point is not to set a definition in concrete but to explore the terrain, not to frame an answer to the question What is ministry? but to deepen and make more profound our questions about ministry. As you read each description, stop for a minute, reflect on each phrase, and see how your idea of ministry agrees or disagrees with the various authors.

Elements that Constitute Ministry

The question of what constitutes ministry is a serious one for seminarians as they are attempting to learn the ropes and develop a sense of themselves as ministers. As I have already said, the elasticity of the word is sometimes stretched to include a casual kind word or gesture that any civilized human being would extend to another, or else it is so restricted that only formal and structured Church-related services are included.

Field-education experiences in secular settings often raise the issue for students. One seminarian's concern grew out of his frustration at not being able to speak "of our hope in Jesus Christ" when ministering to a patient in a hospice. The family was not religious and expected Bob, the seminarian, to provide a gentle presence and to help in the bodily needs of the dying man. In his journal Bob reflected, "I feel as though I have one arm tied behind my back in this situation, because my first instinct would be to talk about our hope in Jesus Christ . . . but if the person doesn't share this hope, then what? In our efforts to minister, are there times when we can only attend to a person's bodily needs? If so, how as a young minister can I get over my eager desire to 'save the world'?"

Secular settings are not the only locus of doubt regarding what is included in ministry. Working in a Church organization is no guarantee that ministry will be more easily defined. Tom worked in the office of the marriage tribunal and was interviewing a witness in a marriage annulment case. In evaluating his participation, Tom wrote:

Jack [the witness] was not resistent to the conversation. I thought his answers were honest, though I certainly got the impression that he thought the process was ridiculous. I tried to be sensitive to him and the issues. It was not easy for me to ask some of the required personal questions. . . . Church as institution certainly determined the juridical format of this conversation. However, I tried to conduct myself remembering that this was a person's life I was dealing with. Jack saw the church as an institution, thought the process was ridiculous but never questioned it. He just went right ahead and answered all the questions. . . . I am left with two questions: How is this ministry? and Does the interview process in itself help people toward God?

Bob and Tom, as well as the rest of us, are responsible for developing a theology of ministry. The good news is that we don't have to do it all alone, nor do we simply have to accept uncritically what others have said. Bob, Tom, and we have resources to draw on.

The questions that arise from pastoral experience are also being addressed by theologians, and their voices need to be included in the discussion. We look to them not for a definite answer or definition but rather for guidance and direction in our own thinking. I will, therefore suggest a variety of thinking on the subject. Ministry, according to the "Report to the 1984 Convention of the Lutheran Church in America" is "the service Christians offer to each other and to the world as well as the proclamation of the Word and the administration of the Sacraments. . . . Ministry is the response of Christians in every sphere of life to the gracious call of God. It is carried out in homes, at work, with friends and strangers, at church, in community and government."[5] Joseph Cardinal Bernardin speaks for many in the Church when he adds another dimension: "Ministry is a specific activity supported and designated by the church, which discloses the presence of God in some way in our human condition and empowers us to love more fully in the mystery of God—in communion with God and with one another."[6]

Thomas O'Meara, O.P., explicitly ties in ministry with the coming of the reign of God: Ministry is "the public activity of a baptized follower of Jesus Christ flowing from the Spirit's charism and an individual personality on behalf of a Christian community to witness to, serve and realize the kingdom of God."[7] The late Urban Holmes III identifies that reign as political. He wrote that ministry is the Church's function to mediate the mystery of God to humanity, supremely revealed in Jesus Christ, in order that human beings

5. "God's People in Ministry: A Report to the 1984 Convention of the Lutheran Church in America," 5.

6. "In Service to One Another," *Origins* (n.d.) 135.

7. *Theology of Ministry* (New York: Paulist, 1983) 142.

might become that for which they were created. The wholeness of humanity demands life, body, and community. Therefore, the goal of ministry is political. Life in the Church is a promise of a redeemed city.[8]

There are common threads drawn through the descriptions of ministry I have listed. Even when specific issues are not included in one statement, there is no implicit denial in others. For instance, the call from God mentioned by the Lutheran statement is not echoed by the others, but neither is it denied. Similarly, the absence of specific mention of kingdom of God is not to be taken as a denial of that aim of ministry. But there is one important point where the statements may disagree. How broadly or how narrowly are we to understand "supported and designated by the church?" I will speak to this issue shortly.

In spite of our inability to agree on a definition of the word, we have enough elements of agreement that we may continue the conversation. I will focus on just four defining notes: (1) Ministry is specific service to persons in need (2) done in the name of the risen Christ (3) rooted in the Church and (4) contributing to the coming of the reign of God.

Service

Professional ministry within the Church has been called "ecclesial ministry." Ministry to the rest of the world has been labeled "outreach ministry." There has been movement on the part of some in the hierarchy to identify outreach ministry as the province of the laity, which of course leaves ecclesial ministry as the province of the clergy. This becomes more problematic in the Catholic Church in the light of the shortage of priests and of our understanding of the baptismal obligation to service within the Christian community.

Outreach ministry may involve organized Church activity or it may involve individual response to people's needs. Catholic Charities, the Home Mission Board, and the Saint Vincent de Paul Society are examples of the first. Dorothy Day, Tom Dooly, and the many persons who respond to the AIDS crisis by setting up clinics and hospices are only a few examples of the second. Christians do not have to wait for authorities to provide the opportunity to serve. Each of us has the responsibility to minister as a result of our baptismal commitment.[9]

8. *See Ministry and Imagination* (New York: Seabury, 1976) 34.

9. In my own Congregation, Providence Houses have been established in convents where sisters welcome women who need a home for themselves and their children. Other sisters have opened their convent homes to mentally handicapped and deaf adults. Still others shelter the homeless from foreign shores.

But ministry is more than attending to the material, psychological, or spiritual needs of others. Government and big business are both involved in the material, psychological, even the spiritual needs of people. Ministry, however, involves attending to the mystery of life and of God's love. It requires that we see the "more than meets the eye" in the events of life. "The meaning of the ministry of the church is always, at heart, the transmission of the meaning of a transcendental experience manifest in the ordinary world."[10]

Ministry helps us and others to recognize the presence of God in the pain, suffering, joy, and delights of human life; thus, ministry goes beyond alleviating pain or celebrating joy. It holds up the pain and the joy to the light of the gospel and demands a response from us in the light of the same gospel. Ministry may be service directly in and for the Church, or it may be in and for the world (and so for the Church). In either case, ministry is always at the service of justice and peace.

Having said that, I am not here encouraging a pie-in-the-sky kind of passive acceptance of pain and suffering. Rather, in seeing pain and suffering in the light of the gospel, we are impelled to respond as Jesus did and to work toward healing, redeeming, and liberating the world from sin and pain and suffering. Because of this gospel mandate, ministry always demands that we measure and weigh our work in the light of justice. "Action on behalf of justice and participation in the transformation of the world fully appear to us as a constitutive dimension of the preaching of the Gospel, or in other words, of the Church's mission for the redemption of the human race and its liberation from every oppressive situation."[11] Demands of justice are *constitutive* of the gospel. We dare not ignore them.

Ministry is not about making people feel better or salving over difficult situations. It often means taking the hard road. "Make-nice" ministry is the result of domesticating the message of the gospel. It has been fostered by a sentimental imaging of Jesus and of his life's work. But Christ's ministry challenges our human tendency to seek the comfortable, settled state of affairs. Jesus did not always make people feel better. True, he healed and forgave, but he also criticized and condemned injustice in the temple and in society. It was not for his miracles that he was crucified but for challenging evil. In our own century, Martin Luther King, Jr., Archbishop Romero, and the martyrs of El Salvador, Jean Donovan, Dorothy Kazel, Ita Ford, and Maura Clark, are stark reminders of the consequences of taking the hard road.

10. Holmes, *Ministry and Imagination,* 262.
11. The Third International Synod of Bishops, "Justice in the World" (Washington: United States Catholic Conference, 1972) 34.

If the aim of our ministry is only to help people to feel better, they are often left in our debt. They are likely to see us and we are likely to see ourselves as their savior, and the hallmark of the relationship may be patronizing. Ministry is then practiced for our own benefit rather than in response to the suffering of others. In that case, ministry works to our downfall, no matter how well we are perceived. It ceases to deserve the name "ministry." The complexity of the issue is evident in a case study presented by a student who was involved in working with poor children and who took a hard line "trying to avoid patronizing the poor by not having some expectations of them. Are we putting them down when we expect less, when out of 'pity' or 'concern' we do not challenge them? Can we be hardliners in some areas— in education, for instance, where we cannot be in others—as with food and shelter?. . . Who are we to push them? Some of my difficulties lie in my desire to be popular with the youngsters."

I would like to say parenthetically here that while the student is concerned about "tough love" and is not primarily concerned about his motivation, a supervisor may use the situation as an opportunity to speak with the seminarian about mixed motives. If we all wait until our motives are as pure as the driven snow, we may never get involved at all. Students' reflections often raise more issues than the one the student is primarily solicitous about.

We have been criticized for a Band-Aid approach to ministry, bandaging wounds that should not have been inflicted in the first place. We have been likened to the man who kept dragging drowning people out of the river instead of going upstream to find out what made them fall into the river in the first place. While it is necessary for us to continue to assist the immediate needs of poor and oppressed people, that can not be the extent of our ministry. Even the most personal and individual ministry must be kept within the context of systemic oppression. We have to find out who or what is throwing people into the river.

I can think of no situation that is outside the realm of ministry. All of creation is connected, and all of creation is in need of healing. Tevye in *Fiddler on the Roof* describes every occurrence of life with at least four or five "on the other hands." So, too, with ministry. Ministry attends to the material, psychological, and spiritual needs of others; on the other hand, it is aware of the "more than," that is, the mystery of life. It alleviates pain and suffering; on the other hand, it recognizes God in suffering. Ministry serves individual women and men; on the other hand, it is ever aware of the political ramifications of personal needs. Ministry is about making people feel better; on the other hand, it is about confronting, challenging, prophesying. Ministry applies Band-Aids where needed; on the other hand, it strives to discover who or what is causing the wound.

In the Name of the Risen Christ

Jews and Muslims do not speak of their good works as ministry. It is a particularly Christian term. "Minister" comes from the Latin *minus*, which means "the lesser one" who comes in the name of the *magister*, the greater one. The minister does not perform good for others only out of some natural disposition toward service or in response to a command from authority. Ministry is a response to the grace of baptism and confirmation. Ministry is a response to the example and challenge of Jesus. It is giving a cup of water in his name, it is doing to the least of his brothers and sisters in his name, it is taking seriously the injunction to do as Jesus did.

Service to others given by a good Jew or Muslim in response to religious motivation is not ministry. If that last sentence is problematic, is it because we are still thinking of ministry in a hierarchical way? Is saying that something is not ministry saying something negative about it? Recognizing the wonderful generosity of Jews and Muslims in the service of God and realizing that they do not call it ministry may be another way for us to crack through the hierarchical mode of thinking about ministry. Saying that Jews and Muslims do not do ministry is not to suggest that ministry is better than what Jews or Muslims do in response to God's love. It is merely to stress that ministry is a Christian word and that others may not appreciate our imposing our language on them.

The minister acts, as did the apostles and disciples, in the name of Jesus. It is for this reason that we can say to one another: "Your faith has cured you. Go in peace." "Be not afraid." "Your sins are forgiven." We have the assurance that all we ask the Father in Jesus' name will be given us. Our ministry does not arise out of our own talents and abilities. They help, of course, but the force, the grace, the unction, of our ministry arises out of our incorporation into Christ Jesus in baptism.

In speaking of ministering in the name of the risen Christ, I am suggesting that it is not enough to revert to the historical Jesus; rather, we are responding to the presence of the risen Christ here and now. The Spirit, present with us today, is the Spirit of Jesus. "It is important for us to rediscover this proximity of Jesus to his Spirit, for ministry is grounded not so much in the imitation of the historical Jesus as in the personal response to his Spirit."[12] Ministry is not an attempt to reenact what Jesus did two thousand years ago but to take his message seriously in this twentieth century.

---

12. O'Meara, *Theology of Ministry*, 48.

Within a Church Context

Christians are not a loose collection of free-lancers; we are a community of faith, which we call Church. The Church, according to Richard McBrien, is "the whole community (assembly) of baptized persons called by God the Father to acknowledge the lordship of Jesus, the Son of God, in word, in worship, in witness and in service and, through the power of the Holy Spirit, to share in Jesus' historic mission for the sake of the Kingdom of God."[13] Membership in the Church calls us to announce the word, to worship, to witness, and to serve, as we acknowledge Jesus as the Son of God. Membership in the Church calls us to attend in our day to the mission of Jesus. Membership in the Church calls us to ministry.

Ministry, as understood in our culture, is a church word. It is a Church activity. Ministry implies involvement in a community. Acting in the name of Christ is acting in the name of the Church. By "Church," I do not mean only the Vatican, deanery, diocese, or parish, nor do I exclude them. I am speaking here of the communal aspect of Church rather than the institutional one. My definition of "Church" and "ministry" recognizes that the work of such organizations as Network, the Women's Ordination Conference, Call to Action, as well as volunteer doctors and nurses in remote areas of the country and the like, may be truly ministry.

In opting for a more communal model of Church rather than a strongly institutional one, I have already determined my response to the question raised earlier about the meaning of "supported and commissioned by the church." Of course, ecclesial ministries by their very nature call for some kind of public support and commissioning by the institution. This may take the form of ordination of the clergy or commissioning of lay ministers. In the Catholic tradition, commissioning has become problematic, since canon 230 specifically states that laymen may be commissioned to the ministries of lector and acolyte but that laypersons may "fulfill the function of lector during liturgical actions by temporary deputation: likewise all lay persons can fulfill the functions of commentator or cantor or other functions, in accord with the norms of law."[14] Throughout the section "The Obligations and Rights of the Lay Christian Faithful," the Latin reads *Christifideles laici* (Christian faithful) or simply *laici* (laity); only in regard to public commissioning is *viri laici* (lay men) used. Because women are denied even this commissioning, the practice of commissioning anyone is falling into disuse in many areas.

---

13. *Ministry: A Theological, Pastoral Handbook* (San Francisco: Harper & Row) 15.
14. *Code of Canon Law* (Washington: Canon Law Society of America, 1983) 77.

Although institutional support and commissioning are not as explicit as they might be, being hired by and receiving a salary from a Church-related hospital, school, university, parish, or diocese constitutes support and even an unofficial "commissioning." Moreover, the various ministries associated with parishes such as baking bread, teaching Sunday School or in a religious-education program, welcoming new members or visiting the sick on behalf of the parish, are accepted and ratified by the community and are rooted in the community that is the Church. The acceptance and recognition by the community constitute a kind of informal commissioning.

But support and commissioning for outreach ministries does not always receive even unofficial or communal recognition. It may arise instead from the very life of the community. Membership in the Christian community impels us to ministry. The values and commitment to service of the community are in themselves the support for ministry. Teachers, social workers, big sisters and brothers, rape counselors, funeral directors, volunteers in nursing homes and shelters for the homeless, and legal aid societies that serve in the name of Jesus and are rooted within the Christian community find the support and confirmation for their ministry within that community.

Toward the Coming of the Reign of God

Ministry is a conscious and deliberate response to the example and challenge of Jesus. Ministry is a continuation of the mission of Jesus, establishing grace and holiness, peace and justice. It is a commitment to bring about the reign of God.[15] This suggests that ministry is not only about particular or individual service to someone in need but that every act of ministry has an impact on the coming of the promised reign of God, the *basileia*. The reign of God is not only some future goal of ministry; it is the present milieu in which ministry occurs. Elisabeth Schüssler Fiorenza gives us some insight into the meaning of *basileia*. As preached by Jesus, it is both present and future, both already and not-yet. "Jesus' praxis and vision of the *basileia* is the mediation of God's future into the structures and experiences of his own time and people."[16] By his life and work, Jesus made visible the coming of the reign of God.

Every human act works either for or against bringing about the reign of God, but ministry is both a *deliberate* and *conscious* effort to mediate God's

15. I have used the expression "reign of God" instead of the more traditional "kingdom of God" in order to avoid exclusive language.

16. *In Memory of Her* (New York: Crossroad, 1983) 121. *Basileia* eliminates the monarchical language of kingdom or reign of God. Its very foreignness forces us to stop and reconsider what "reign of God" may mean.

future into the structures and experiences of our time and people. That reign of God, toward which we are working, "exists wherever and whenever the will of God is operative, wherever and whenever the will of God is fulfilled . . . as broad and as overarching as the will of God is broad and overarching."[17] By the will of God, I do not mean some concrete plan or blueprint God has for us; rather, the will of God is God's purpose for us, God's intention of peace and justice on earth as it is in heaven. It is God.

Even the most individual and particular ministry is aimed not only at serving a person in need but also at making God not more present but more readily recognized by us. The "already" aspect of *basileia* reminds us that God is present long before we arrive. It may call a halt to the language of "bringing God to people." We might remind ourselves that even in the desert on the way to the Promised Land, God went before the Hebrews and was there before they arrived. We minister not to bring God but to recognize and help others to recognize God's presence among us.

Neither ecclesial nor secular service *in itself* is ministry. The act of ordination is no guarantee that the service performed is ministry, nor is it a guarantee that everything an ordained person does is ministry. We must finally recognize that ministry is not better, holier, more sanctified, or more sanctifying than other works. Service becomes ministry when it is done in the name of the risen Christ, is confirmed by the Christian community, and contributes to the coming of the reign of God. When that motivation is missing, the work may still have the same or better results. It may enhance the coming of the reign of God, but I would not call it ministry, since it is not done deliberately and consciously, nor is it rooted in and confirmed by the Christian community.

Does this suggest that we need to be conscious and deliberate about every action, every response, every service we perform? Of course not. We don't expect wives and husbands or men and women in religious congregations to remind themselves constantly of the vows they have taken. Commitments in marriage or in religious congregations are meant to free us. Our deliberate and conscious choice simply needs periodic renewal. Keeping the spotlight on ourselves and our motivation is unnecessary navel gazing and uses energy better spent in ministry.

The Ministry of Supervision

The clergy and laity who are involved in the field supervision of seminarians are involved in a profound ministry not only to the individual student

17. McBrien, *Ministry,* 19.

but to the Church at large. By preparing Church leaders, supervisors of ministry students are preparing the Church itself for the next millennium. Supervision is a ministry that is already forecasting what the Church of the future will look like. It is one of the ministries that does not follow hierarchical lines; it is undertaken by both clergy and laity without differentiating titles. It depends on discussion, dialogue, cooperation, and collaboration. It is mutually supportive and challenging. Clergy supervise clergy and laity, and laity supervise future ordained and nonordained ministers. Each contributes according to giftedness, not according to role or title. Supervisors are involved in helping candidates for ordination to minister in a more collaborative way, and they are helping lay ministers to accept the responsibility that is theirs by virtue of their baptism.

As a result of ministry students' field work in the community, more and more of the local clergy and laity are involved in the formation of future ministers and priests. More and more of the clergy and laity are teaching ministry students the skills needed in ministry; more and more of the clergy and laity are recommending or not recommending that the seminary consider these students for ministry. And more and more of the local clergy and laity are bringing their theological insights and questions to bear on the academic study of theology. The end result is not just that the face of ministry is changing but that the face of theology is changing too.

Ministry is some specific service to persons in need done in the name of the risen Christ, which is confirmed by the Church and which contributes to the coming of the reign of God. Supervision, then, may be ministry. I say "may be" because I have already suggested that not all good works are ministry, not all ecclesial works are ministry. As with other good works, supervision of ministry students *in itself* is not ministry. It is service, confirmed by the Church in the guise of the seminary or university; it contributes to the coming of the reign of God. But when supervision is a response to the call of the Spirit, when it is done in the name of the Risen Christ, when it is a response to the gospel, then it is ministry.

Service

It has happened that when seminarians are assigned to a parish or a hospital, the staff sees them as free or cheap help. Since most ministers I know are overworked, they welcome a few more hands. But that is not what field work is about. Ministerial field education is about the training and preparation of Church ministers in cooperation with an experienced minister who agrees to act as supervisor. Supervision is serious work that involves a commitment to pass on the skills, the knowledge, and the wisdom to the next generation of ministers, as well as a commitment to the development of creative and critical analytic skills.

Supervision is activity on behalf of another, in this case, of a ministry student. The supervisory relationship exists for the benefit of the student. It is a gift from an experienced professional to a neophyte. It goes without saying that it is also direct service to the Church itself.

In the Name of the Risen Christ

Field education is not just about polishing pastoral skills. The most significant aspect is theological reflection. Supervision is one of the places where academic theology and practical theology come into conversation. It is one of the places where seminarians attempt to bring their professed and operative theologies into alignment with one another. In supervision, seminarians are given the opportunity to articulate what they believe and to reflect on their behavior to see how congruent the two are. It would seem impossible, then, that supervision could function well without reference to the life, teaching, and death of Jesus. "The Program of Priestly Formation" (see Appendix) discusses at length the importance of theological reflection in the ministry students' learning process.

Confirmed by the Church

When a hospice worker, a Christian educator, or a pastor agrees to supervise a seminarian, that person enters into a covenant relationship with the seminary or university. He or she is commissioned by those institutions to assist in the education of future Church leaders, whether that commission is made explicit or not. Directors of field education are very careful and full of care about the men and women they invite to supervise the seminarians.

While the invitation to supervise is a form of commissioning, it would be better if there were a liturgy of commissioning. In that very ritual we would remind everyone involved—students, supervisors, and seminary staff—that the supervisors are partners in the work of the seminary. Whether a supervisor is engaged in ecclesial ministry full time or not, supervision brings her or him into that fold. It is a Church activity.

Toward the Basileia

Can we doubt that anything we do to improve ministry in the future will foster the reign of God? The students with whom we work are the future leaders of the Church. They are the ones to whom congregations will look for guidance, for healing, and for challenge. They are the ones who will be responsible for the prayer and ritual of the community. It is they who will preach, teach, baptize, confirm the community, bury the dead, and console the living. They are the ones who will minister to the disenfranchised, the oppressed, the despised of society.

One of my challenges to supervisors is, "Would you believe what this person preached about the word? Do you want him to teach your children about God? Do you want her at your deathbed?" It is my way of reminding them of the profound significance of their work. Long after many of us are gone, these young women and men will be serving God and others. It is up to us to make sure they are as well prepared as they possibly can be.

Points for Reflection

1. Write your own description of ministry. In the light of that statement, would you understand supervision as ministry?

2. How significant is "commissioned by the church" in order for a service to be called ministry?

3. How can we help the laity better understand that baptism and confirmation call them to ministry? How can we help the clergy better understand that?

4. How can we balance concern for ministering to immediate needs with concern for the systems that produce those needs?

5. How have your ideas about ministry changed in recent years?

6. What do you understand by the phrase "ministry is to foster the reign of God"?

Chapter Three

Supervision as Education

Education, like ministry, is a word that has suffered from two extremes: It has been stretched to a point where it encompasses everything, and it has been restricted to mean only what occurs in schools and universities. Before we can talk about supervision as education, we need to be clear how we are using the word "education" here.

Paulo Freire, one of the most significant educational theorists of this century, has taught a generation of educators that there is no such thing as a *neutral* educational process. Education is either an instrument to integrate students into the logic of the dominant system and to bring them into conformity to it, or else it is "the practice of freedom." It is then a means by which men and women deal critically and creatively with reality and are empowered to participate in the transformation of society.[1]

In the light of these words, it is no accident that I choose to discuss supervision under the name "education." Supervision is not a neutral process; it is an important means of enabling future ministers to deal critically and creatively with ministerial situations and where they learn to participate in the transformation of society, or in more theological language, to help bring about the reign of God.

In the past, the procedure was called "field work" or "field experience," but students and supervisors easily lost sight of the purpose of the experience. Neither work nor experience capture the essence of education seen as the practice of freedom. Supervision is the catalyst that transforms work and experience into education. Supervision enables seminarians to deal critically and creatively with reality and to discover how they might participate in the transformation of the world, in the coming of the reign of God. But because it does not follow the traditional form of education, it has sometimes not taken seri-

---

1. *See* Paulo Freire, *Pedagogy of the Oppressed* (New York: Herder and Herder, 1971).

ously enough the theories and principles of education. No matter what role the supervisor plays in the community, whether pastor, chaplain, social worker, or counselor, when a supervisory relationship is established, the role is that of teacher in that relationship.

Please don't conjure up visions of your first-grade teacher, Miss Jean Brodie, or Mr. Chips. They were teachers of children and adolescents and were more or less successful as they knew and tried to understand children and adolescents. But theories about childhood learning are not appropriate in a discussion about how adults learn. Think rather of Castaneda's Don Juan or Obi Wan Kenobi of *Star Wars* fame or Shug in *The Color Purple*—teachers, mentors who journeyed with another in their search for wisdom.

I will follow the pattern typical of education literature, discussing the learner, the teacher, the process, and the curriculum. The education we are talking about is the education of adults, and we will be more or less successful as we know and understand how adults learn. Let us therefore turn to some of the theorists concerned with how adults learn in order to learn how better to supervise.

A Look at the Learner

Adult education may be defined as a process whereby women and men undertake systematic and sustained learning activities to attain new knowledge, to acquire desired attitudes or values, or to develop certain skills. It is the adult student who undertakes the learning experience, who chooses what is to be learned, what knowledge and wisdom are to be pursued. Malcolm Knowles, one of the best-known theorists, begins with the ancient insight that the heart of education is learning, not teaching. He places the focus first on the adult as learner and only then on the teacher. Knowles identifies four basic differences between the education of children (pedagogy) and the education of adults, which he calls "andragogy."[2] They are differences in self-concept, in experience, in readiness to learn, and in orientation to learning.

Self-concept

Children understand themselves to be dependent on adults. They experience security when parents, relatives, and teachers can be depended on.

2. Andragogy is derived from the Greek root *andr* (adult) and *agoge* (the activity of leading). Andragogy is thus the art and science of helping adults learn. The word has come under some criticism, since the root *andr* is more properly translated "man" rather than "adult."

They need direction and support appropriate to their years. But as they mature and become psychologically adult, they achieve a self-concept of essential self-direction. Adults react with resentment and resistance when they find themselves in situations where they are not allowed to be self directing. An experience in which adults perceive themselves as being treated like children is bound to interfere with their learning.

Ministry students may be younger and less experienced than their supervisors, but they are mature adults who are responsible for their own lives and learning. It is our privilege to cooperate with them in the endeavor and to offer another model of education than the one to which many of us, as well as they, have been subjected and which has been the subject of much criticism. "For much of this century, theological education has tended to educate and form people to be dependent rather than independent, to be reactive rather than intentional, to be so absorbed in satisfying the expectations of other people and systems, i.e., canonical procedures, course distributions, bishops, deans and professors, that the learner has had little time or energy left to take any initiative or responsibility in the education-formation process."[3]

The best gift we can give our students is to assist them in their journey toward greater independence, intentionality, and responsibility. The aim of the supervisory relationship is to bring the student to parity with the supervisor, to lessen the "inequality" between supervisor and supervisee.

Jean Baker Miller distinguishes two kinds of relationships of inequality. Relationships of permanent inequality such as slavery exist for the benefit of the superior person or group; dominant people define roles for themselves and for subordinates. Services they do not want to perform are relegated to the inferiors. In this situation subordinates develop qualities that are pleasing to the dominant group and that will, therefore, make their lives more bearable. "These characteristics form a familiar cluster: submissiveness, passivity, docility, lack of initiative, inability to act, to decide, to think and the like. In general, this cluster includes qualities more characteristic of children than adults—immaturity, weakness, and helplessness. If subordinates adopt these characteristics they are considered well-adjusted."[4]

In contrast, relationships of temporary inequality exist for the benefit of the "lesser." "The 'superior' party presumably has more of some ability or

3. George I. Hunter, "Theological Field Education and Its Relationship to Seminary Curriculum, the Church and Ministry" (unpublished "occasional paper," Divinity School of the Pacific, Berkeley, Calif., January 16, 1986.
4. *Toward a New Psychology of Women* (Boston: Beacon Press, 1976) 7. The language "immaturity, weakness, and helplessness" is not meant to characterize children negatively but to suggest that some characteristics appropriate in children are inappropriate in adults.

valuable quality, which she/he is supposed to impart to the 'lesser' person. While these abilities vary with the particular relationship, they include emotional maturity, experience in the world, physical skills, a body of knowledge, or techniques for acquiring certain kinds of knowledge.''[5] Supervision certainly comes under the definition of temporary inequality, and like parents, doctors, teachers, and others involved in such relationships, supervisors work toward their own obsolescence. The period of inequality is meant to be temporary; the goal of the relationship is to end the relationship as it exists. The persons involved may still continue their involvement, but they will be peers, friends, colleagues, enemies, or competitors.

The trouble is that some people learn to be good "lessers." Some because of a fear of the consequences, others because people in power often do not know how many rights to "allow" the lesser or how much power they ought to have or how much they may act on their own perceptions. In either case, it is difficult for the lesser to make the journey from lesser to full stature. Ministers who are overly dependent and who see themselves as inferior to others disvalue not only themselves but other people whom they may perceive as inferior. Paulo Freire insists that persons who disvalue themselves disvalue others like them. Horizontal violence, treating those most like us as we have been treated, is the result. The minimizing of dependence has consequences not only for the individual involved but for others who will come into her or his sphere of influence.

Experience

Working with adults is trickier than working with children. If it is important to deal with children as distinct individuals, it is even more so when dealing with adults. Their different life experiences have marked them even more significantly than children and affect how and what they learn. But whether twelve or thirty-five or fifty years old, each person we encounter deserves to be treated as an individual, not as a stereotype. Awareness of theories and principles and systems is not a substitute for genuine and respectful meeting.

Seminarians tend to be more experienced than they were in the past; for a significant number, ministry is a second career. Some have experience as teachers, nurses, service men and women, parents, or ministers. They bring a wealth of experience with them, which provides a basis for new learning. The life experience of the students is a resource for learning. Their ministry

5. Ibid., 4. *See also* the discussion of temporary and permanent inequality, pp. 4–12.

at the field site is a continuation of their life experience and will be understood in the light of that experience.

A neophyte in a hospital is there to learn how to heal and how to console, but healing and consoling have been part of every adult's life. Many women in mid-life return to school or begin to work outside the home. The universal phenomenon is not how little they know but how much they know. Perhaps their wisdom and knowledge went unnoticed because it was not named by them or by others. Persons who know only middle-class suburbia have much to learn from people who know how to survive and grow in an inner city. But suburbanites are not devoid of life experience. They also have something to teach as well as to learn as they minister among the poor.

But just living for a certain number of years does not insure "experience," as it is used here. The experience must be lifted up, reflected upon, examined, measured, and finally incorporated into the new knowledge that is being constructed.

Readiness to Learn

We speak of "teachable moments" as the peak times when people are best able to learn. Events of life open us to the possibility of learning what was of no interest to us before. Parents of newborns experience many teachable moments. They learn to care for another human being totally dependent on them. They learn to relate to one another in a new way. They perceive life, the world, God, differently than before. In its sacramental programs for parents before the baptism of their child, the Church teaches what women and men were probably not ready for before. Moving, getting a new job, coping with illness, loss, or other problems, falling in love, these are teachable moments when women and men are ripe for learning.

Seminary and university life is or should be full of teachable moments, and among the most significant of these is the time spent at the field site. This is not at all to suggest that we wait for a student to develop a desire for a particular learning. We may model for them the values and relationships appropriate to ministry; we may focus their attention on necessary skills or desired behaviors; we may inspire them to new understandings of ministry. But in the long run the student is the one who is responsible for his or her own education. The students will decide what will be learned, what will be valued, what will be incorporated into their being. We cannot take that responsibility from them, or we risk a generation of dependent "lessers."

A perceptive supervisor-teacher recognizes the teachable moment sometimes when a student does not. Meeting a homeless person for the first time, sitting with a grieving parent for the first time, or counseling a drug addict for the first time dislocates and disorients many students. That dislocation is a teachable moment. Questions about personal and societal responsibility, questions about an all-loving God, and questions about sin and grace and free will may be raised by the supervisor if the student is not already wrestling with them.

Sometimes the dislocation is so painful that supervisors avoid the distress that would accompany probing the situation. The following is taken from a report written by Donna, a seminarian whose field setting was a rape-counseling center. She herself was a rape victim who had not reported the crime. In a training session with the police, one officer displayed a negative attitude toward women, referring to a rape victim as "the scene of the crime." He also emphasized that the chance of getting a conviction was very low and that plea bargaining occurs without the consent or knowledge of the victim. Donna wrote:

> When the session was over, I was angry and totally frustrated. I decided that I could never advise a victim to go through the process, with little hope for a conviction and the possibility of being revictimized by the system. . . . When I met with my supervisor, she challenged me on my position. Was I letting my own bias get in the way of giving fair advice? She asked me to reevaluate what I would say to a victim that would be honest and yet not scare her away from reporting. She helped me to avoid letting my own strong feelings get in the way of giving good counsel to a woman.

The supervisor enabled Donna to work through her life experiences, her convictions, and her biases. In so doing, she "helped me integrate these feelings and experiences so that they will be a gift in my ministry rather than blinding me to those to whom I minister." It may have been easier for the supervisor to reassign Donna to different work at the center. Instead, she struggled through the pain and grief with her and helped her to learn in the midst of her dislocation.

Orientation to Learning

Children learn for the future. They study to get promoted, to get into high school, to graduate, to be accepted into college. The curriculum is therefore subject-centered. It is organized into courses and sequenced in a logical way.[6]

---

6. I am not suggesting that this is the best way for children to learn. Many innovative theories more in line with what Knowles describes for adults are being successfully used with children.

Andragogical learning, however, is problem-centered. It is a process of focusing on a problem and searching for some solutions. By "problem" we mean some goal, some needed skill, some recognized lack that needs to be addressed in the here and now. It presumes that the student is actively involved in the direction of her or his education, not a passive participant waiting to see what someone else thinks is important to learn. It is not that the student alone determines everything in the learning process. Rather, the process will be more beneficial if the student is involved as an experienced adult struggling with a problem at a teachable moment.

When Paulo Freire speaks of problem-posing education, he opposes it to what he calls "banking education." In banking education, the teacher deposits and the students receive, memorize, repeat, file, and store information. "In the banking concept of education, knowledge is a gift bestowed by those who consider themselves knowledgeable upon those whom they consider to know nothing."[7] Problem-posing education is not about learning to react to crisis situations but rather is about understanding crises as opportunities for change, for transformation. In problem-posing education, students develop an ability to perceive the world not as a fixed reality but as a reality able to be changed, transformed. It may require a progression from a worldview that blames God for all that is to a worldview that holds each of us responsible for recreating the earth. Such an education helps us to realize that we create the future as we move with the Spirit.

In summary, then, the seminarian is a responsible adult with a wealth of experience (some of which is not yet reflected upon and therefore not yet accessible as educational). Moreover, the seminarian is involved in the pursuit of ministerial skills and is therefore at an eminently teachable moment.

The Supervisor as Teacher and Learner

While the student is the main consideration in the learning process, supervisors as teachers also deserve our attention. Before you read on, take a moment to reflect on one or two good teachers you have had in your life. Taste the moment when they touched your being with some new wonder, some exciting idea, some challenging vision. Make a mental list of the qualities of a good teacher. You probably will come up with many that educational theorists propose. Theorists are, after all, people who organize and systematize the wisdom and knowledge of their time.

Supervisors serve as a kind of mentor for students. Mentors hold up a mirror in such a way that the student may see what was not visible before.

7. Freire, *Pedagogy of the Oppressed*, 58.

They offer a more detached way of viewing a situation; they select elements of the story to highlight, they reflect back to the student a new image. Mentors affirm the student's experience and insights while challenging them to newer heights. Mentors are able to develop a relationship based on trust that enables students to develop the courage to let go of what they no longer need and to hold fast to what they do need. The role of the mentor (supervisor) is characterized as supporter, challenger, and provider of vision.[8]

Supporter

Support includes such things as the kind of listening that goes beyond mere hearing, staying alert to what is being said both explicitly and implicitly, providing enough structure so that the student is able to achieve but not so much that the student is stifled. Mentors also support by having positive high expectations of the students. They encourage initiative on the part of the student, they affirm talents and abilities, they encourage new endeavors, risks. Mentors are also advocates, making connections, introducing students to others in the field, helping the student find a place on the staff. Mentors share their own lives, values, and dreams with the student.

Challenger

But support is not enough. In fact, by itself, it can lead to a kind of unthinking complacency that does not foster growth and learning. Mentors also challenge. They introduce alternative ways of seeing a situation, point to missed pieces, connect fragments that seem disparate. They offer " 'cow plops' on the road to truth—that raise questions about the students' current world views and invite them to entertain alternatives, to close dissonance, accommodate their structures, think afresh."[9] If learning is closing the gaps, then teaching that is challenging is opening up gaps. When I asked my students to consider one piece of advice they would give supervisors, challenge was the overwhelming answer. "Challenge us! Encourage us to explore the full potential of whatever ministry we are involved in, to really 'try it on' to see if it fits." Challenge those you supervise to grow deeper within themselves as well as in ministerial skills.

8. Laurent A. Daloz, *Effective Teaching and Mentoring: Realizing the Transformational Power of Adult Learning Experiences* (San Francisco: Jossey-Bass, 1986) 212–235.
9. Ibid., 223.

Provider of Vision

Offering a vision is helping the student to see—not necessarily what the mentor sees but to see more clearly what lies beyond the horizon. Mentors understand that vision includes sight, insight, and foresight. They help the student to see what is present, to develop some insights about that present, and to place it in relationship with the future, to foresee. "Mentors 'hang around' through transitions, a foot on either side of the gulf; they offer a hand to help us swing across. By their very existence, mentors provide proof that the journey can be made, the leap taken."[10]

The teacher-supervisor I speak of is one for whom dialogue with students is a sine qua non. I speak of a teacher who is not a banker, depositing information to be filed away for future use. The educator I speak of is one who knows that in dialogue the student becomes teacher and the teacher becomes student. Time and again supervisors have said to me that in their discussions with seminarians they have learned even as they taught.

The Process

"Dialogue is the encounter between [persons], mediated by the world, in order to name the world."[11] To name the world, for Freire, is to change it. And the naming can only occur in dialogue. Dialogue is intimately related to praxis, action-reflection. We shall speak more about this point later in this chapter.

Freire lists five characteristics that facilitate dialogue. The first is love. The encounter in dialogue is to rename the world, to change it. Such a profound task demands a profound love, a love for all humanity and for the world itself. "Because love is an act of courage, not of fear, love is commitment to other [human beings]. . . . As an act of bravery, love cannot be sentimental; as an act of freedom, it must not serve as a pretext for manipulation. . . . If I do not love the world—if I do not love life—if I do not love men [and women]—I cannot enter into dialogue."[12]

Micah 6:8 challenges us "to act justly, to love tenderly and to walk humbly with God." Sharon Parks offers an explanation of Yahweh's tender love, which will shed light on our discussion. The meaning of *ahah* and *hesed*, which is captured in the translation "to love tenderly," is "like Yahweh's covenant love, continually calling us into a new and more faithful being;

10. Ibid., 213.
11. Freire, *Pedagogy of the Oppressed*, 76–81.
12. Ibid., 78.

it is love that reaches out to us not only tenderly but also tenaciously.''[13] It is a love that is manifested not in sentimentality but in justice.

The second requirement for dialogue is humility. "Humility" comes from the same root as *humus,* soil. We have sometimes misinterpreted that connection because of our disrespect for the earth. We thought humble meant being lowly, even as we saw the earth to be lowly. But to be really humble means to realize from whence we have come. We have been created from the earth, which the Creator saw as good. Humility helps us to cherish the realization that we are one with Mother Earth, and the consciousness of that connection serves to keep us truly humble—one with the earth and with others.

It is impossible to dialogue if one party considers that the other is ignorant with nothing to contribute. It is impossible to dialogue if I do not perceive my own brokenness, my own ignorance, my own lack of wisdom. It is a sheer act of arrogance to enter into a discussion with the purpose of convincing others that I possess the truth and will bestow it upon them. In true dialogue, neither perceives the other as ignorant nor themselves as the font of wisdom. They are persons coming together to learn what they do not yet know.

The third quality necessary for dialogue is faith—faith in our fellow human beings, faith in our joint ability to make and remake the world, and faith in our vocation to be more fully human. Faith means neither certainty nor security. It is more like letting go of one trapeze and standing firmly in midair between two trapezes, trusting that you will be caught.[14]

Hope, the fourth quality, follows faith and love even as the seasons follow one another. If we have no hope that anything will come of our dialogue, then the meeting can only be frustrating and sterile. Hope, according to Freire, is rooted in our incompleteness, in our search that is carried on in communion with others. It is all well and good to love another, to have faith in them, to be humble with them, but little will be accomplished for either one without some sense of hope, some sense that the present reality is full of possibilities and that we are the stewards of those possibilities.

Hope is not a naive optimism. It is hard reality. Augustine knew that when he wrote, "Hope has two lovely daughters: anger so what should not

13. Sharon Parks, "Love Tenderly," in Walter Brueggemann, Sharon Parks, and Thomas Groome, *To Act Justly, Love Tenderly, Walk Humbly: An Agenda for Ministers* (New York: Paulist, 1986) 39.

14. Jack McCall shared this image with his class at Boston College in 1974. It is one of the many things he taught that I have held on to through the years.

be will not be and courage so that what should be will be." Hopelessness robs us of the passion of righteous anger and quiet courage.

The last characteristic of true dialogue is the ability to engage in critical thinking. "Finally, true dialogue cannot exist unless the dialoguers engage in critical thinking . . . thinking which perceives reality as process, as transformation, rather than as a static entity—thinking which does not separate itself from action, but constantly immerses itself in temporality without fear of the risks involved."[15] The following suggestions of patterns for supervision have been chosen because each takes critical thinking seriously.

The Curriculum

We have looked at the seminarian as learner, the supervisor as teacher, the process as dialogical; now it is time to investigate what the curriculum may be in this process of supervision. The word is derived from the Latin *currere* which means "the course to be run." It suggests a track with a beginning and an end. It suggests that the purpose is to finish the race. It suggests something that can be measured and quantified. It suggests a relationship between time and space in which covering the greatest space in the least time is the best way to go.

Elliot Eisner presents another view of curriculum for our reflection: "The curriculum . . . can be conceived of as a series of planned events that are intended to have educational consequences for one or more students."[16] The events are planned, not haphazard, and planned with the intention of educating. Supervisors often assign ministry students specific duties because that is what has to be done at the time. But the point of field education is not to accomplish what needs to be done in the parish or agency but rather to plan events so that the student can learn. It is expected that the work assigned will benefit the ministry, but that is not the primary purpose of the student's participation. The point of the whole endeavor is the *student's education*.

In discussing educational consequences, Eisner speaks of three distinct curricula: explicit, implicit, and null. The explicit curriculum is what it is that we plan or intend to happen. In field education, the goals and objectives of the student (more about them later) are part of the explicit curriculum. Such things as learning the skill of active listening or the art of open questioning, learning to counsel, to teach, to preach, to lead a group, learning when silence is the best conversation.

15. Freire, *Pedagogy of the Oppressed*, 80–81.
16. *The Educational Imagination* (New York: Macmillan, 1979) 39.

The kind of knowing most appropriate to this process has been called "connected knowing." It differs from the separate form of knowing common in academia. Separate knowers attempt some objectivity, they search for loopholes and contradictions. They are "especially suspicious of ideas that feel right; they feel a special obligation to examine such ideas critically, whether these ideas originate in their own heads or come from someone else."[17]

In contrast, connected knowers try to share the experience of others in an attempt to gain access to the others' knowledge. "Connected knowers do not measure other people's words by some impersonal standard. Their purpose is not to judge but to understand."[18] Connected knowers befriend the experience; they know in an intimate way. Perhaps the biblical notion of knowing, *yadah*, says it best. The word is used in the sense of knowing something "by heart" or "with the heart"; it also means to know in a sexual way, to be one with one's beloved. This model of connected knowing applies on many levels in our discussion. The student tries to understand the welfare client or the teenager on drugs; tries to discover what poverty, illness, lack of education, pain, despair, can do to a person. The supervisor tries to know what the student feels, sees, questions.

But more happens in an educational setting than is planned. The implicit curriculum includes those things that have unintended educational consequences. The way the staff or team treats one another, the way clients are spoken of, how authority is used, how creativity is accepted, what is celebrated, what mourned—all are facets of the implicit curriculum. The budget is a facet of the implicit curriculum. The architecture, the art, the music, the presence or absence of beauty, are facets of the implicit curriculum.

I am on the board of the Advocacy Center in South Bend, Indiana; it is the center of last resort when all other avenues seem closed to poor people. The Center is always short of money, always poor even as the people they serve are poor. When I first joined the board, I suggested that instead of contacting churches as each need arose, it would be a good idea to ask each church to send a donation each month so that the Center would have a fairly decent working budget. It was a suggestion born of my efficient nature. But the Center values direct contact between the churches and the people whom they help. It values the personal touch. It values having the ministry students who serve there know what it is to be without resources, having to ask

17. Mary Field Belenky and others, *Women's Ways of Knowing* (New York: Basic Books, 1986) 104.
18. Ibid., 116.

for what is needed. It values being poor with the poor. Those values are part of the implicit curriculum, more valuable in that setting than efficiency.

There is another curriculum that needs our attention, and that is the null curriculum. "And we can identify the null curriculum—the options students are not afforded, the perspectives they may never know about, much less be able to use, the concepts and skills that are not a part of their intellectual [or emotional] repertoire. . . . Their absence will have important consequences on the kind of life that students choose to lead."[19] Periodically we need to ask ourselves, What is being left out of the supervisory relationship? What topics are avoided? What issues are ignored? What questions left unexplored? Authority, obedience, sexuality, male-female relations, race, the economy, all impinge on ministry. All therefore should be deleted from the null curriculum and become explicit in the discussion.

Some Suggestions for Supervision

There is no one perfect way to supervise, but I would like to propose three models that may enhance the learning process suggested by the call for dialogue and critical thinking. The first was developed by Tom Groome, the second by Joe Holland and Peter Henriot, and the third by Evelyn Eaton Whitehead and James Whitehead. Only Groome presents his models under the formal rubric of education, but the other two clearly fit into a discussion of education as I have described it.

Shared Christian Praxis

Thomas Groome describes the shared Christian praxis approach as "a group of Christians sharing in dialogue their critical reflection on present action in light of the Christian Story and its Vision toward the end of lived Christian faith."[20] Groome speaks of five moments of shared Christian praxis. The first is naming present action. This movement is geared to elicit an expression of a student's feelings, sentiments, beliefs, relationships, and the like. It does not ask for a theoretical defense from an expert. The question may be, In what way did you minister today? How were you ministered to? What was exciting, frustrating, challenging, nourishing, disappointing, in your ministry today? It may be as simple as, What did you want to bring

19. Elliot Eisner, *The Educational Imagination*, 92.
20. *Christian Religious Education: Sharing Our Story and Vision* (San Francisco: Harper & Row, 1980) 185. The five moments of shared Christian praxis are described in pp. 206–232.

to supervision today? The questions are not meant to be threatening or valuative but to invite reflection. The process begins with personal experience,
confirming that God is indeed at work in each life.

The second movement deepens the reflection. "But while critical reason
begins by noticing the obvious in the present, at a deeper level of reflection
it must delve below the obvious. By a critical valuative analysis we can attempt to discover the interest in the present action, critique the ideology that
maintains it, and recognize the assumptions upon which it is based."[21] The
second movement concerns the student's stories and visions. Why are you
doing ministry? What are your hopes, your dreams, in what you are doing?
It is at this point that memory and imagination play a significant role. What
led you to ministry? Why are you committed to ministry to battered women,
to youthful offenders, to the dying? Why do you think you feel so strongly
about the situation? This movement is designed to go beyond a superficial
understanding of the present situation and to discover how one's past, one's
social and cultural influences, affect behavior. We try to connect the present
reality with a larger story. But the past and the present are attended to in
order that a different future may be envisioned.

I was once with a group of professors who were discussing the contributions of some long-term veterans of our profession when someone said that
a colleague had taught forty years at the same institution. Another replied,
"No, he taught one year forty times." Lack of reflection on our present practice results in repeating our successes and failures over and over. This second
movement is designed to focus the spotlight on what and why we believe
and how and why we behave as we do in order to create a new future.

The personal story and vision does not stand alone. The third moment
is the encounter with the Christian Story and Vision. At this point, Groome
suggests that the teacher present in a dialogical way the Christian Story and
Vision, being faithful to the broader community's understanding of that story
and vision, being careful not to make his or her own version sound like the
final statement of the "truth." Since in supervision we are working with students who are studying and reflecting on the Christian Story and Vision in
a structured way, we might ask them to be responsible for this step. What
in the life of Jesus speaks to this problem? What model of Church (institution, community, servant, herald, sacrament, disciple, etc.) supports what
you are doing? Do the recent encyclicals, pastorals, and other Church documents challenge you in this situation?

Telling one's story is one thing, and listening and reflecting on the Chris-

21. Ibid., 185.

tian story is another. The point is to bring them into conversation. The connection must be made. This fourth movement flows readily from the third as I am proposing it. What do the two stories have to say to each other? The conversation goes in both directions—individual experience and the Christian story have something to learn and something to teach each other. This is not a time of examination of conscience, searching personal behavior to see where it has failed the scriptural or Church model. The movement is in two directions: Experience is informed by the Christian Story and Vision, and the lived faith experience informs and contributes to that story.

Groome calls the fifth movement the "Dialectical Hermeneutic Between the Vision and the Participants Vision"—an academic phrase asking how what we are involved in is a sign of and contributes to the coming of the reign of God. It is the movement that impels us to action. How will what we have discussed influence your future behavior in similar situations? One aim of supervision, like an aim of good education, is to empower the student to make decisions wisely. Sometimes ministry students will choose a path that we would not. That is their responsibility and right. There is no one perfect decision, no absolutely right way. In our respect for our students, we trust that they are being faithful to their understanding of the Christian Story and Vision. Theirs may be the more faithful rendering of that story and vision.

These five steps are not steps of a ladder, which must be taken in order, but are more like steps of a dance, which often follows a sequence, repetition, and tempo of its own. They demand fluidity, openness, a willingness to change direction, even to dance backwards sometimes. But they are not steps in a solo performance. The process requires that we have at least one partner in the community willing to move through the music of our own lives as it harmonizes with the gospel.

I once heard Tom Groome give a homely example of the process. Young Christopher came running into the house crying, and his father asked, "What happened?" (first movement). "Eileen hit me," was the teary reply. After wiping away the tears and giving Chris a hug, Daddy asked, "How did that make you feel?" (second movement). After Chris confessed to feeling mad, hurt, and would never speak to his cousin again, his father reminded him of the good times he had had with her and how much they loved one another. Even God loved Eileen! Besides, Mommy and Daddy often forgave Christopher when he made them angry (third movement).

Putting the memory of the love of parents and God for himself and his cousin, even when he misbehaved, into conversation with his own hurt is the fourth movement. But the process is not over until future action is decided upon. "Now what are you going to do?" (fifth movement). While the father certainly had his ideas about what Christopher should do, the boy was given a degree of freedom to decide when and if he would play with Eileen.

The Pastoral Circle[22]

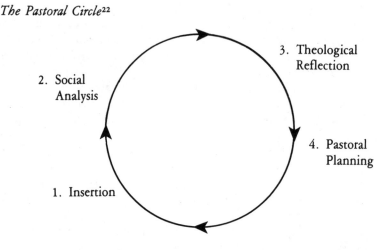

3. Theological Reflection

2. Social Analysis

4. Pastoral Planning

1. Insertion

Joe Holland and Peter Henriot, leaders in the search for a just world, did not list the four moments in a column; instead, they chose a circle to suggest that the process is ongoing. After passing through the four stages, we are back to a new beginning where we must start the process over again. It is a process that does not allow us to sit complacently and believe that we have found the truth. Again, the movement of the dance suggests itself. The action is graceful, fluid, moving back and forth between steps.

Experience is the basis for the analysis. The first moment is insertion into the lived experience of individuals and communities. People's feelings and responses to what is happening in their lives constitute the data for reflection. Taking people's experience seriously as the locus of religiously significant information demands that we reflect on them from a firsthand perspective. It suggests that we heed "the signs of the times." In Matthew 16:1-4 Jesus criticizes the Pharisees and Sadducees who tried to entrap him. They knew how to read the skies and determine whether to expect fair weather or stormy. But they could not read the signs of the times. They had no eyes to see nor ears to hear what God was revealing in the lives of the people. They were not really inserted into the life of the community. Suggested ques-

22. Joe Holland and Peter Henriot, S.J., *Social Analysis: Linking Faith and Justice* (Maryknoll, N.Y.: Orbis Books, 1980) 7–30.

tions at this point are, "Where and with whom are we locating ourselves as we begin our process: Whose experience is being considered? Are there groups that are 'left out' when the experience is discussed? Does the experience of the poor and oppressed have a privileged role to play in the process?"[23]

Maria Harris shares a story two of her students told her about their experience in a women's correctional facility. Their experience of being locked up for only five hours forced them to reflect on three questions. "The questions were: 1) What did you hear today? 2) Why did you hear what you heard? (What in your background, your history, your culture, your bias, your prejudice caused you to hear what you heard?) And 3) What didn't you hear? What didn't you allow yourself to hear?"[24] They were trying to immerse themselves in the lives of the women in prison. They were taking seriously the challenge to begin from the perspective of those with whom they minister.

Insertion is followed by a critical analysis of the situation. Data gathered from the economic, social, political, and cultural arenas are analyzed to discover linkages, to identify causes, and to plan for action. We remember that the personal is political and ask, Who benefits from the situation? Who pays for it, economically, physically, psychologically, or spiritually? Who wins? Who loses? How did the system, institution, situation, develop? What values are exhibited?

I spent a semester in India, and while I was there, I had the good fortune to stay at a school for blind women. The sisters taught the women the fine art of weaving, and these sightless women produced magnificent fabrics they would never enjoy. They also formed a beautiful choir and even performed intricate Indian dances. One Sunday, the women gave a concert and reception for some benefactors, and when one of the guests asked why there was so much blindness, one sister immediately responded, "Low wages." She had done her homework. She knew that parents who are exploited and underpaid cannot feed their children and that malnourished children suffer from sickness and premature death. She made the connections between personal pain and systemic injustice.

But social and cultural information is not enough. The next step is to question what all this means in the light of the gospel and of our understanding of the gospel as spelled out in the social teachings of the Churches. What do the Exodus, the Resurrection, the psalms, and the parables have to teach us in this situation? In our ministry, we try to give God a place to

---

23. Ibid., 9.
24. "Field Education as Parable," *Report of the Proceedings of the Twentieth Biennial Consultation of the Association for Theological Field Education* (Association for Theological Field Education, 1989) 19.

be seen. But we must see God in that place first. We must reflect not only for ourselves but that we may be able to reflect God to others more clearly.

Since this is a praxis model, it does not end in reflection but demands action. Not precipitous action but carefully planned and executed action. The questions here are, How might things be different? What can we do to make them different? It takes seriously the obligation to action, but just as seriously, the obligation for intelligent action. What do we think will really facilitate change in an oppressive situation? What can we do to heal, redeem, and liberate? What is the ministry to which God is calling us to?

I have purposely chosen to situate the discussion of dialogue in the context of praxis and social analysis to insure that supervision-teaching will not become domesticated, tamed, safe. Even though the matter for a particular session of supervision may be the problem of one teenager or one widower, the dialogue needs to keep alive the social, political, and cultural connections. Otherwise, ministry may become merely a series of reactions to crises, a running about to put out the fires, applying Band-Aids when radical surgery may be called for.

Tripolar Model

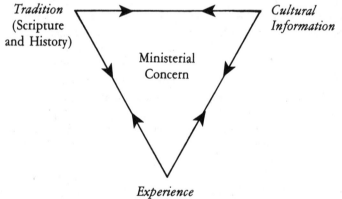

The insights of Evelyn Eaton Whitehead and James D. Whitehead[25] put into conversation and into tension three sources of theological reflection: Chris-

25. *Method in Ministry: Theological Reflection and Christian Ministry* (New York: Seabury, 1983).

tian tradition, experience, and the resources of the culture. Christian tradition includes Scripture and Church history; experience, the individual and community's awareness of a particular ministerial concern; and the resources of the culture includes the language, symbols, mores, and sciences of a people. This tripolar model, as originally designed by the Whiteheads, is geared to enable a community to address important and complex pastoral issues. I am suggesting that it is also a good model for supervision, whether between two persons or within a group.

Experience. Like the models of Holland, Henriot, and Groome, the process begins here. The lived experience of each one and of the community as a whole is the locus of God's activity. The ministry student's lived experience is the first place where he or she meets God. Unless the seminarian is conscious of that, books, lectures, and rituals will have no effect. The challenge of this pole is that a recent ministerial experience itself is reflected upon, critiqued. The feelings, ideas, convictions, prejudices, hopes, and dreams of the student are neither accepted without examination nor are they discounted. Self-knowledge grows from and deepens from the process. Students also learn that their experience is colored by their culture and history, even as the experience of the community in which the student ministers is colored by its culture and history. The matter of dialogue is both the student's experience and the student's perception of the community's experience. The notion of the sense of the faithful, the *sensus fidelium*, is active; think of it as a verb. It is not the Christian community's passive regurgitation of what has been taught by the institutional Church. Learning to recognize the sense of the faithful presupposes that the student is involved more than superficially with a reflecting Christian community.

In supervision, the student presents a concern that grows out of a ministerial experience. Journal entries, verbatims, and case studies are but a few of the possible tools for the presentation. Current involvement in ministry is the meat of the supervisory session. The on-site experience is the beginning of the conversation. Together, supervisor and supervisee examine the experience, not for flaws but for insights about how to minister better. This does not involve just an account of what happened. More importantly, How did it affect the student? What questions need exploring? What feelings have to be understood? It also opens the conversation about how things may have been done differently.

Tradition. Tradition is not to be thought of as an unchanging package of information passed from one generation to another. "Traditioning" may be the better way to think of the process, since a verb rather than a noun describes what is meant. Each generation is part of the traditioning— accepting, critiquing past understandings and contributing its understand- ing of the Christian message, and, in turn being critiqued by it. Tradition is varied, sometimes at odds with itself, enigmatic. Right from the begin- ning the four evangelists give us different perspectives; in different times and places there have been a variety of understandings and expressions of our faith. A case has been made for slavery, charging interest on money has been condemned, women have been defined as "defective males." But we be- lieve that tradition has both divine and human elements at work. Tradition is both an embarrassment of riches and a scandal. "[The dynamics involved in a reflection on tradition] is one of preserving and overcoming: preserving the gracefulness of the theological and pastoral choices of our tradition while overcoming some of the limitations of their formulation."[26]

The Whiteheads speak of befriending the tradition, not mastering it. Their befriending is similar to connected knowledge, which we discussed earlier. It is more than an intellectual grasp; again, *yadah* may express it best. Tradi- tion includes not just Scripture, the theses of theologians, and the Church documents; it also includes the understanding of the faith of past Christian communities—the *sensus fidelium*. Tradition will not provide the answers to students' questions. It provides the parameters for solutions; it gives them the space in which to search for solutions. It is not that they are looking for the one true solution to life's problems. If there were only one true answer, certainly someone would have found it by now. But that is not God's way with us; each of us and each generation struggles and learns, in the light of both tradition and experience. In engaging tradition in conversation, the seminarian places himself or herself in line with the saints and sinners of our past in order to understand what the present is demanding.

Cultural Information. In the recent past, the Church and the world were set in opposition to each other, engaged as enemies in a battle, the forces of God on one side and the forces of Satan on the other. But we have lately returned to an appreciation of culture that does not identify all good with the Church and evil with the world. The title of the Pastoral Constitution on the Church in the Modern World expresses our renewed understanding— The Church *in* the modern world, not the Church *and* the modern world. The theological implications are that the Church and the world mutually af-

---

26. Ibid., 16.

fect each other. The culture has been Christianized even as the Church has been touched by the insights and wisdom of culture. Like tradition and experience, culture is both positive and negative. At times holy, at times demonic, at times ambiguous, culture has a unique contribution to the process of faith sharing.

The findings of sociology, psychology, and anthropology are especially valuable in helping ministers to understand the effects of economic and political decisions from a ministerial perspective. Students who have worked at the shelter for the homeless or the Advocacy Center have been led through careful supervision to make connections between corporate decisions and poverty. They have seen firsthand the effects of poverty on children's ability to think, to learn, even to play. Students at the shelter for battered women discover linkages between lack of education, low self-image, lack of family or community support, and a tolerance for being abused.

But it is not to the social sciences alone that we may turn. Artists of all sorts—musicians, poets, painters—often express the understandings of a culture years before theologians are able to. The music of the civil rights and peace movements predated statements by the various denominations on race and peace. The poetry of the children of the Holocaust contains insights theologians are still struggling with. Social scientists provide us with knowledge about human psychology and the nature of community. Other religious traditions affirm and challenge our own faith. Amateur theologians like Woody Allen and Lily Tomlin struggle with eternal verities, Charlie Brown preaches profound sermons, Alvin Ailey's "Revelation" is truly revelatory.

At the same time, our culture fosters competition, individualism, selfishness, consumerism, and lack of commitment. "The pole of cultural information thus represents not a realm of unredeemed nature, but a mixed environment, partly antithetical to and partly complementary to Christian life."[27] Awareness of the culture means knowing the economic, political, and social realities of the people. It may mean knowing who the decision makers are; it means knowing and appreciating the music and the art of the people. Awareness of the culture means focusing on evil in society, but it also means recognizing those hints of grace that are often missed.

There is overlapping among all three poles. The separation is for the purpose of discussion, but we need to remember that none exists except in relationship to the others. Culture, human experience, and tradition continually play on one another, for better and for worse. The *sensus fidelium* is colored by each, hence the need for honest and humble critique of each of the poles.

27. Ibid., 19–21. Citation is on p. 21.

The similarities among the three models are obvious. I offer all three because the subtle differences allow for a wider range of opportunities in supervision. At times, shared Christian praxis, setting the student's story and vision into conversation with the Christian Story and Vision may be most helpful. At other times, the social analysis demanded in the pastoral circle may be more appropriate. Still other times may benefit by the tension between tradition, experience, and culture in the tripolar model.

Whatever process you choose to use in supervision, I am suggesting that it is imperative to keep in mind that in supervision you are working with mature adults who have the right and obligation to be actively involved in their education. Further, the supervisory relationship is both dialogical and structured. It is not casual and informal conversation, but, like all good education, supervision is a deliberate, conscious attending to an issue in such a way that the learner teaches and the teacher learns.

Points for Reflection

1. Do you think education is a good model through which to understand supervision?

2. In what ways can you guard against supervisory relationships that keep students in the position of "lesser"?

3. What qualities, besides those listed, describe a good teacher?

4. Look at your ministerial setting. What is it implicitly teaching? What do the furnishings, the atmosphere, and the people implicitly suggest that the parish or agency is really about?

5. What issues are usually consigned even if unconsciously, to the null curriculum? Do they belong there?

6. What issues do we usually avoid in supervision? Authority? Sexuality? Male-Female conflicts or differences? Others?

7. What tensions were at play for you as you began the task of supervision?

Chapter Four

Supervisory Artifacts

It is not easy to learn an art. Learning to weave, play a musical instrument, or create a painting, sculpture, or a piece of pottery means first learning the very basics. Only then can you attend to the fine points, to the spirit that gives life to the artistic rendition. Would-be musicians learn the scales, but that is no guarantee that they will produce music. Sculptors practice with stone and wood and metal, but their work does not always result in art. In my pottery class, we learned and practiced the basics about clay; only then did the teacher speak to us of the subtleties of line, shape, color, and form. We had to achieve some rudimentary skills before we could attend to the niceties that an aesthetic appreciation bestows. And that is what makes all the difference.

So it is with the artifacts of field education. There are basic skills to be learned, but that is not the whole story. In the hands of those who shape and form them well, they become works of art. In this chapter we will discuss some of the artifacts that facilitate theological learning at the field site. Most if not all field-education programs require some variation of these, and students usually have some competence in them—some students are well versed in their use, others need more help and guidance. I am speaking of the student's covenant/contract, journal, case studies, and critical incidents and of the supervisor's feedback and evaluation.

Contracts, journals, and case studies are included in the process as educational devices, but they are meant to be valuable lifelong assets for the students. They are the primary responsibility of the student, but the supervisor, like a good guide, assists in the process. It is therefore important for supervisors to know why contracts and journals are required and how they may be used for the benefit of the student. If a student draws up a covenant/contract, keeps a journal, or develops a case study simply because one is required, then I would almost rather that they did not do it at all. (I say ''almost,'' since I think the discipline of meeting requirements is in itself good learning.) The written work is not for the benefit of the field-education director or the supervisor. It is not required simply to be filed for future reference. All of the documents are designed for the benefit and growth of the seminarian. They are live documents, not dead records. Anything you can do to use them in that way will profit the student. We will also discuss the report or evaluation that the supervisor is asked to submit to the seminary.

Covenant/Contract

In most relationships the responsibilities, privileges, rituals, and expectations fall into place almost unnoticed. We rarely verbalize our commitment to a relationship except in cases that are ratified publicly, such as marriage, legal contracts, and religious vows. We function in everyday life with unwritten contracts, agreements. We may have pledged in childhood or adolescence that we would be someone's ''best friend,'' but as we approach adulthood we ordinarily do not contract friendship. If we are lucky, we recognize at some point that friendship has happened between us.

But there are some relationships that are more formal, more structured toward a desired goal, where expectations are best made clear. Supervision is one of those relationships. Whether the language of contract or covenant is used determines, in part, the expectations of everyone involved. Contract has a more legal sense; it stresses requirements, rights, and duties. Covenant echoes the language describing the relationship between Israel and God. Since I will be talking about what contract and covenant have in common, I will use the words interchangeably, even though I believe they carry different connotations. One practical benefit of the contract is that it places the supervisory relationship on a more objective footing, focusing attention on the work to be accomplished. That focus may be one of the drawbacks of contractual language; it smatters of the legal, emphasizing obligations, suggesting sanctions. Covenant language is more subjective; it conjures up the notion of commitment and promise. And that, too, may be both a plus and a minus. Supervision is, after all, a relationship between persons and often deepens and matures beyond contractual guidelines. But if too much attention is focused on the relationship itself, the focus of supervision, which is the ministerial activity of the student, may get lost.[1]

---

1. *See* William J. Clost, ''The Learning Covenant as Institutionalized Functional Theology,'' *Practical Theology and Theological Reflection,* ed. Donald F. Beisswenger, Tjaard Hommes, and Doran C. McCarty (Association for Theological Field Education, 1984) 68–74.

Whether the document specifying expectations is called contract or covenant or internship agreement-form, the general purpose is the same—to spell out precisely what the student can expect at the field site and what the site can expect from the student. Contractually, the student expresses a commitment to undertake theological study for ministry in a particular field setting. The covenant/contract is first and foremost the student's responsibility, but since the supervisor is more familiar with the placement, input and feedback are very important. Students sometimes do not know what goals may be realistic and possible in specific settings. The supervisor can help focus goals, can explain what is expected of the student at the setting, and can help to make the contract a true learning opportunity. The supervisor, in signing the contract, agrees to help the student to carry it out.

Contracts, like Gaul, may be divided into three parts: a description of the pastoral setting, the student's goals and objectives, and a description of supervisory expectations. There is no one best way of writing a contract or covenant, but most models will include the following considerations.

Describing the Setting

Many ministry programs provide a listing of the various approved settings for field sites. Each parish and agency describes, in a short paragraph, its purpose and philosophy. It also describes the position open to divinity students. The description often gives a taste of the setting. One parish was listed in our booklet as "the best parish in the area." That did attract students' attention. These descriptions not only help the students to choose a placement, they are helpful in writing this first section of the contract, where the student's responsibilities regarding the rest of the staff and parishioners or clients are carefully spelled out. It is important to include the days and the number of hours of involvement each week, as well as the holidays and termination date. The covenant should also include any financial arrangements, such as stipends or travel expenses, that may be involved. The contract keeps both student and supervisor centered on the educational aspect of the field work. It functions best when it forms a backdrop for the issues the seminarian brings to the supervisory sessions. Contracts are also the basis for any evaluation or reporting required by the seminary or university.

Goals and Objectives

The presumption under which I operate is that the seminarian has chosen a site primarily for two reasons: to focus on a particular ministry and to learn or polish the skills appropriate to that ministry. Setting clear, specific goals improves the chance of attaining the skills and attitudes desired. Occasionally, students are unfocused or unclear about specifying what it is they intend to learn. Involvement in ministry without attending to goals is tantamount to being involved in reactive ministry, waiting to see what crisis will arise and then attending to it. Proactive ministry (still open to the exigencies of the day) is a better model from which to operate. Students, therefore, are better served if we can help them to clearly and succinctly state where it is they are heading.

The student is the one who plays the major role in the setting of goals. Authority figures, including supervisors, are not responsible for what learning will be sought. Of course consultation with the supervisor and the field-education director play a part in deciding on learning-goals, as do curriculum requirements and the student's time schedule. But a student-minister is ultimately responsible for his or her own learning and "must be willing and prepared to take major responsibility for the education-formation process in the midst of a system and people who are used to 'caring for' and controlling others."[2] In our desire to be nurturers, we are sometimes tempted to assume the responsibility that belongs to another. We then encourage what Jean Baker Miller has called "lesser" behavior.

My experience with ministry students impels me to advise all supervisors to be a "brake" of sorts to the goals that students set for themselves. Seminarians are idealistic, full of energy and expectation. They want to save the world, eliminate pain and suffering, and have it all done by Sunday. They are often too demanding of themselves and as a result sometimes overburden themselves and taste failure unnecessarily. Focusing aims and setting realistic goals is one of the first contributions a supervisor can make. I have never had to advise a student that their goals were too easy; I have never had to suggest that perhaps they were being lazy or inattentive. My job and the job of any supervisor is to help the students set realistic, attainable goals so that their energy may be well spent.

A goal is a statement of purpose. It may indicate just what the student intends to learn or what the student intends to contribute to the setting. I am not suggesting that these two facets of the field work do not overlap and influence, but for purposes of clarity, they are spoken of separately. A goal is a broad statement of what the student hopes to attain—neither so broad as "save the world for Jesus" or "become an experienced campus minister"

2. George I. Hunter, *Supervision and Education-Formation for Ministry* (Cambridge, Mass.: Episcopal Divinity School, 1982) 16.

nor so narrow as "teach every fourth grader to memorize the Ten Command-ment and the Beatitudes" or "preach on justice six times."

I insist that students write goals by saying "I will . . . ," not "I would like to . . ." or "I hope to . . . ." The very writing in that way seems to strengthen the commitment. If we say "I will get a home run," not "I want to get a home run" or "I hope I get a home run," our chances are better that we will hit one over the fence. Of course, "I will" is not a guarantee, but it is stronger than "I hope" or "I want to." And, of course, even if I hit a home run, there is no guarantee that the game will be won.

Goals may be professional (What do I want for myself out of this ex-perience?) or project (What am I willing to contribute in this setting?). Pro-fessional goals are those skills and abilities that the student wishes to learn. They are a reminder that the student is at the field placement primarily to learn—learn through ministry, yes, but learn. Professional goals may include such things as, "I will develop better listening skills." "I will be more asser-tive in expressing my beliefs." "I will be less aggressive in my relationships with the opposite sex." Professional goals are often expressions of ideals that will have to be worked on for years or a lifetime.

Project goals may include such things as, "I will improve the parish music program." "I will minister to hospice patients and their families in a com-passionate manner." "I will develop a youth program for Resurrection par-ish." While students may choose a field setting in order to develop some specific professional goal themselves, the project goal usually depends more on consultation with the supervisor. Since the supervisor is the person who knows the needs of the parish or agency better, it is not possible for a stu-dent, new to the placement, to set realistic and appropriate goals alone. As I have mentioned, supervisors can be especially helpful in keeping goals manageable and attainable.

As anyone who has ever decided to go on a diet knows, goals alone do not do the trick. We have to set up very specific steps toward reaching the goal. These specific steps are objectives. Objectives flow from goals. An ob-jective is a statement that focuses more precisely on the general direction in which a person is heading; it provides the specific steps that will be taken to attain the goal. Objectives are concrete, measurable, attainable.

For example, if my professional goal is to improve listening skills, some objectives may be, "I will read three articles on the art of listening." "I will maintain eye contact when speaking on difficult subjects." "I will get the advise of my supervisor concerning leading questions. I will ask Chaplain Costello (who has the reputation of being a good listener) if I might accom-pany her once a week on hospital rounds." "I will not interject my own sto-ries and experiences but keep focused on the patient."

If my project goal is to serve St. Mary's parish through the RCIA program, my objectives may be, "I will participate in the weekly staff preparation meetings." "I will meet with each catechumen individually each month." "I will prepare three presentations for the group."

Suppose your goal is to develop a better understanding of the relationship between ministry of the ordained and professional lay ministry. Write your own objectives! Keep them concrete, measurable, and attainable.

We do not always accomplish our goals. Students are not judged by their success or failure to attain their goals, but they can be held accountable for carrying out their objectives. They may never get to hit that home run, but they can be expected to show up at practice, eat a balanced diet, get enough sleep, exercise, and whatever else the coach demands. So too with ministerial goals. In a discussion of goals, there can be a difference of opinion as to whether or not the goal was attained. A supervisor may recognize improvement in interpersonal skills, but the student may still be disappointed in the progress made. He or she may think, "I am a little better, but I am not there yet." Not so with objectives. Questions about objectives can usually be answered with a yes or no. A student and supervisor can go down the list and answer whether each objective was carried out. That is where the responsibility of the student lies.

This part of the contract/covenant may be checked for adequacy by using the SPIRO model.[3] The acronym stands for "specificity, performance, involvement, realism, and observability." Specificity demands the contract be in concrete terms; contracts are not the place for pious platitudes or fuzzy phrases. Performance lets us know exactly what the student will be doing; it is essential that those expectations are clearly understood by everyone involved. Involvement spells out the extent of the seminarian's activity in the placement: Is the student expected to become involved in extracurricular activities at the parish? To attend liturgies? To socialize with the staff? Realism insures that the goals are attainable within the time limit; young people are often impatient with the slow process of life and set unreal demands on themselves. We help hold their feet on the ground even as their spirits may soar. Observability suggests that it ought to be obvious to the student and others involved whether or not the objectives have been carried out and progress made toward the goal.

3. SPIRO was developed by Claus Rohlfs and cited in Doran McCarty, *The Supervision of Ministry Students* (Atlanta: Home Mission Board, Southern Baptist Convention, 1979) 145.

The Supervisory Sessions

The third part of the contract treats of supervision. The student, in consultation with the supervisor, decides on a particular mode of supervision (apprentice, resource, consultation, etc.). The place and time of the supervisory sessions is recorded in the contract. Both should be carefully considered. A busy office with the phone ringing and people coming in and out is not the best setting. Neither is the kitchen. Squeezing in an hour between two important meetings is not the best time. In fairness to the seminarian, the time and place of supervision should suggest the importance of the meeting. Interruptions should be held to a minimum and then only for emergencies. Since supervision is ministry, the supervisory hour deserves as much respect as any ministerial conference.

Before I speak about a structure for supervisory sessions, a word about the initial session. Since you will be sharing some profound discussions with the student, it is only fitting that you get to know something about each other: likes, dislikes, family, schools, interests, motivation, hobbies—almost anything that makes a human contact and begins to build an atmosphere of trust. Most important is to discover why the seminarian has chosen your particular parish, hospital, center, or agency. Without prying or being judgmental, find out what makes the student tick. Listen with your third ear, be attentive to what is behind the words being said. That, of course, is good advice for all the sessions.

It is not enough for you to get to know the seminarians; introduce them to the rest of the staff, include them in conversations with the parishioners. Better still, publicly introduce them, perhaps at liturgy or a public meeting, put their names in the parish bulletin, make them visible and welcome. The more the seminarian is included as part of the community, the better the experience.

The supervisory session is not an informal chat, a coffee klatch, or a social dinner conversation. It is a formal, structured, professional discussion with an agenda determined by the student. Students are ordinarily required to keep a ministerial journal. A helpful practice is to have the student present a written account of what is to be discussed at least one day in advance of the meeting. The journal entry sets the agenda; it is the starting point for the discussion. Having it ahead of time gives you a chance to prepare for the discussion. Journal entries may take the form of case studies, critical incidents, verbatims, or simply reflections on issues of concern.

Some supervisors respond to the students in writing—a word or two of support or challenge in the margin, a suggestion of an article to read. Reading the student's remarks before the meeting gives you the opportunity to formulate more probing questions, to highlight parts that the student may be overlooking, to consider the issue. This is a very important facet of supervision. An unreflective response, one that seems too spontaneous or thoughtless, may be interpreted by the seminarian as superficial or without sufficient understanding of what is shared. When I asked my students what was most frustrating for them in supervision, they had a variety of responses, but the only one that was listed more than once was "a supervisor who does not read my journal, who comes to the session unprepared, who spends the hour trying to catch up."

The written material will be part of the student's ministerial journal and should be returned to the student promptly. As the discussion begins, you may have some clarification questions about the facts of the particular journal entry. When both you and the student are satisfied that the situation is understood, you are able to move to the level that focuses on the seminarian's feeling and emotional response. "How did you feel about that? . . . How do you handle anger, frustration?. . . What encourages you in ministry? . . . What would you do differently? . . . ." Experienced supervisors know that the questions should not only focus on the negative but should highlight what attracts the student to ministry. The supervisory sessions are not confession or chapter of faults. Questions are not tricks or accusations but opportunities for students to articulate their responses to serious issues, to examine their motivation, and to develop their theology of ministry. Often the first few questions are trial balloons, discovering just what a student is willing to put into the discussion and what he or she hopes to get out of it. But the discussion does not end at the feeling or emotional level. Theological reflection is a constitutive element of ministerial supervision.

I do not want to give the impression that the main function of the supervisor is to ask open or leading questions. Sharing insights, stories about your own beginnings in ministry, wisdom you have learned over the years, also play a part. But your role is not to lecture; it is to respond to the concerns of the seminarian, to interpret situations from another perspective, to provide alternative views, to call attention to recurring themes, to point out strengths and inconsistencies, but especially to support, encourage, and challenge.

Ministerial Journal

I have mentioned the journal a number of times, but a few remarks may be helpful here. I encourage the students to keep a folder for their field-education materials. These might include parish bulletins, announcements, pictures, notes, and any materials their supervisor shares as well as their own written remarks. Including such things seems to make the journal itself come to life and gives a flavor of the setting. They set it in a context. The journal is, for some students, difficult to learn, but for those who are faithful to it, the journal becomes a source of greater self-knowledge.

No matter how articulate a person is in expressing an idea or describing a situation, journaling slows down the process and often leads to surprising results. The journal is a ministerial journal, not a personal one. The entries concern incidents, reactions, reflections about the ministerial experiences of the seminarian. They are the matter for discussion and for theological reflection. Of course the student has the right to withhold any entries from the discussion, but that would probably be a rare occurrence, since one of the points of the journal is to set the agenda for the supervisory session. You might suggest that a student write a case study or a critical incident or that he or she address some issue that you think needs addressing. In any case, the journal is of the student's design.

Case Studies[4]

A case study is a report, usually written, that presents an event involving a dilemma or problem for consideration. It is a slice of life, a recounting of an actual human situation. The Harvard Business School, whose name is almost synonymous with the use of case studies in business education, maintains that a case study presents an issue or problem about which reasonable people may disagree. It is one person's recollection of what happened told as accurately and honestly as possible, but which cannot therefore be taken as "the truth of the matter." Other persons involved may give different accounts. But it is that one person's recollection, and as such it may be a source of learning, especially for the person involved. Professionally and scientifically constructed case studies are beneficial in other teaching and learning situations, but in the relationship of supervision, the ministry of the seminarian is the focus, and the case studies that arise from that ministry are most useful.

A case study is not an account of an extraordinary event in ministry but rather of one that is fairly typical and which involves some responsibility on

---

4. For case studies designed for churches *see* Anne Stenzel and Helen Feeney, *Learning by Case Method* (New York: Seabury, 1970); Kieth Bridson and others, *Case Book on Church and Society* (Nashville: Abingdon, 1974); *Cases in Theological Education* (Case Study Institute, 1981).

the part of the student. Sometimes beginning students look for the uncommon and unique situations; they look for the exciting, the crisis situation. Experienced ministers know that ministry is not always unusual. It is often unexciting and is only infrequently of crisis proportions. Cases that focus on the ordinary are probably more helpful for reflection, since the student will meet similar situations in the future and can prepare for them. Case studies are written in the first person and include four elements: background information, a brief description of what happened, analysis, and evaluation. Sometimes, to protect confidentiality, fictitious names are used.

As in any narrative, the student acts as editor, shaping the incident (perhaps even unconsciously) to focus on the issue at hand. If helpful, snippets of the conversation, as remembered, may be included. This verbatim gives supervisors some insight into how students interact with parishioners and clients and what looms as important to them. Even "doctored" verbatims shed light on what is important to the writer. In the analysis section, the student states just what it is they see happening, paying special attention to the interpersonal dynamics at work. What are the issues, the difficulties? What gave rise to emotions or feelings? Evaluation attends to the unresolved questions the student is left with and / or how the student might have handled things differently.

Ordinarily, a case study should take no more than two pages. This assures that irrelevant information will be eliminated and that the important issues will surface more easily. The discipline of separating the significant from the merely interesting is a useful one. Together, the supervisor and supervisee study the case to identify why the issue is a critical one, to search for alternatives, and to root theological reflection in the concrete experience. It is helpful to discuss how the student may act differently in the future or to reinforce suitable behavior.

Sample Case Study

Background: The parish has been supporting the local battered women's shelter. The Social Action Committee is responsible for parish outreach, and one of the members, Ms. A., who is active in Right to Life, is concerned whether or not the parish is indirectly supporting abortion in supporting the shelter. She and two other members of the committee have spoken with the director and felt that she was evasive on the question. It is the end of a long meeting and everyone is eager to get home.

Verbatim:

Chairperson: Well Folks, what do you think? What should we do? If we can't get a straight answer about their stand on abortion, maybe we shouldn't be funding the shelter.

Me: I really don't know—I believe they are doing a lot of good work and would hate to see us pull out because one person is being evasive with us. The center is in a funny position because so many different religious groups support it and they have different positions on the issue.

Ms. K: I agree. Maybe I am just more liberal but I just can't see deciding this on just one issue. The shelter does a lot of good and it promoted good will between the different churches involved.

Ms. F: (a volunteer at the shelter): I feel the same way. I'd continue to stay there even if the parish pulled out.

Ms. A: Well, I just don't see how we can continue supporting an organization that may be involved in advocating abortion. I know there are two people on the board there who are active in Planned Parenthood.

Mr. A: Yeah, I think we need to be careful about sending the wrong signals. What would the bishop say?

Me: But it seems that the shelter is trying to take a "no stand" position on abortion. If abortion is advocated it would be because some person working there does it, not because the shelter itself is taking a stand for abortion.

Chairperson: Well, we don't have to decide this tonight. We won't actually be disbursing new funds until next year. Why don't we continue to look at the way this develops and make a decision when it is time to talk about next year's budget?

Interpersonal Analysis: Perhaps I should not have jumped in so quickly with my view but it did not prevent anyone who disagreed with me from expressing their views. It was the most honest some of the committee members had been with one another. Also, we allowed the meeting to come to an end too soon. It was late and we were tired.

Theological Analysis: What I had learned in ethics class about formal and material cooperation with evil came flooding back to me. It seemed to be a concern for all the members, some thinking we were giving that cooperation and not considering the importance of witness value of taking a strong stand against abortion. Others didn't seem to think our support constitutes cooperation with evil. I am left with the question about how much I should try to influence people's decisions. Also, should we make the decision not to support an important work on the basis of this issue?

I have asked two supervisors how they would handle this case, what issues would they raise. One thought that it would be important for the student to be clear about his views on abortion. While he didn't think that that would solve the dilemma as presented, it would give the student a firm base from which to speak. The other thought that the significant question was not where the student stood on abortion but rather what should be a minister's responsibility to a group in which opinions are so divided. What skills are needed in leading a group to a decision? Would it be possible to speak of consensus? She also thought that avoiding the issue by putting it off until next time was worthy of discussion. Was it prudence or cowardice? Both supervisors agreed that the student's questions would be foremost in the discussion and the supervisors' insights offered as alternative views.

You may want to take a few minutes to decide what issues you would want to direct attention to. Think in terms of affirmation and growth, not false praise but sincere confirmation. Think also of growth points. Avoid thinking of changing or converting the seminarian; avoid nitpicking; avoid presenting one way as *the* way. I believe the more positive the discussion, the more beneficial it is for the student. After all, the topic is ministry, the student is planning to spend his or her life in ministry. These sessions can encourage and enlighten.

Critical Incidents

I tell our students that whatever distracted them on the way home from their field site is grist for the mill of critical incidents. If they find themselves going over and over some incident or reviewing a conversation frequently, there is usually something significant at issue. A critical incident is one that elicited strong feelings and emotions, one that concerned an issue important to the seminarian. It has been my experience that the incidents that seem the most personal at first are the most universal in application.

One such incident brought by a seminarian to a theological group-discussion concerned getting one's hands dirty in ministry. The incident occurred when the agency in which Brian was ministering had run out of funds. It was November, and a client whose electricity had already been shut off was about to have her gas shut off also. Brian called both utility companies and found out that it would cost fifty dollars to have the electricity turned on but that the gas company would accept a small payment and a promise to continue payments.

> I initially advised her to pay her gas bill; at least she would have heat. Then, as she collected some money she could work toward getting her electricity turned on. The idea of sitting in complete darkness with her kids didn't excite her too much, and it didn't really sit well with me either. The fact that someone would have to make that kind of a decision began to bother me a great deal and so I began to look for other options. One was to "play the system." I looked for ways to manipulate the welfare system in order to benefit Susan. One way was to have her begin a payment plan with the gas company, then divert all her money to get her electricity turned on. Once that was done, she would only have to hold on for twelve days until the moratorium on shutting off utili-

ties went into effect. If her utilities were on, no matter how in debt she was, the utility companies would be unable to shut them off until the spring.

Normally I am wary of clients who play the system so well that they end up abusing it. In a way I had to make a choice between what was just (Susan taking responsibility for her plight and getting on a payment plan she would stick with) and what I thought was compassionate (getting her gas and electricity on no matter what). I decided to present her with this option along with others and allow her to choose. I don't know what she did.

Here is a situation in which the best solution to my client's problem was to "abuse" the system. How appropriate is it for me to present all the options that might be available, even if some of them appear unjust? Did I let my emotions get in the way?

In a discussion on this incident, the conversation ran the gamut from Sartre's problem of "dirty hands"—our involvement in systemic sin—and our benefiting from the systems we criticize to what it means to make ethical choices and to help others to make ethical choices.

Not all the responsibilities belong to the students. Supervisors are responsible for feedback, confrontation, and evaluation. The words themselves sound ominous and out of sync with the rest of this discussion. While much ministry and education are best effected in a positive and supportive atmosphere, we need to attend to the whole human situation. And human situations are sometimes not all sweetness and light, but no matter how difficult, they may be constructive and fruitful for everyone involved.

Feedback

Throughout this discussion, I have been focusing on the support, encouragement, and challenge that supervisors owe supervisees. Perhaps we need a few more words on what I referred to previously regarding mirroring back to students some of the characteristics of which they may be unaware. We all have habits and mannerisms that our friends know well and of which we are unaware. Some are good and others questionable. We do not have the same view of ourselves as others; we see from a different perspective. With the advent of audiotapes, videotapes, and Cam cameras, we have had the unique and often unsettling experience of seeing and hearing ourselves as others see and hear us. We notice those mannerisms and habits of which we were oblivious. We are able, as it were, to step outside ourselves and see ourselves for the first time. Some of what we see is pleasing, but some is not so. Teachers and preachers who video classes and homilies get the students' and the congregations' views. It is often quite different from what they expected.

Supervisors play a more significant role than the audiotape or videotape. Through feedback, supervisors are in a position to let students see how others perceive them. But feedback is not an objective standing outside and viewing oneself from the perspective of the camera lens. Feedback is a process whereby our behavior is interpreted for us in the light of the effect it has on other human beings. We all have a blind spot, some part of ourselves, some facet of our being, which others can observe but of which we are unaware.

When we think about what we know and do not know about ourselves, we may discover that there are four ways of thinking about that knowledge. These are: (1) things that both we and others know about ourselves, (2) things that only we know, (3) things that others know and of which we are unaware, and (4) things that neither we nor others are conscious of. This pattern has been described as the Johari⁵ window after Joe Luft and Harry Ingham, who devised it.

	Known to me	Not known to me
Known to others	I Known to both	II My blind spot
Not known to others	III My secret self	IV Unknown; hidden from both

A supervisor may move some of the information from quadrant II, the blind spot, to quadrant I, known to both. Students may choose to reveal some aspect of their personality or their life to a supervisor, thereby moving infor-

5. *See* Joseph Luft, *Of Human Interaction* (Palo Alto, Calif.: National Press Books, 1969); Philip C. Hanson, "The Johari Window: A Model for Soliciting and Giving Feedback," *The Annual Handbook for Group Facilitators* (University Associates, 1973).

mation from quadrant III to quadrant I. In most relationships the object is to enlarge quadrant I, but not everything belongs in quadrant I. There are appropriate and inappropriate disclosures. We all avoid people who want to tell us, for our own good, of course, every little wart they detect in us. We also avoid people who want to disclose more about themselves than we are prepared to handle. Inappropriate intimacy is no intimacy at all. Blind areas are not all bad, and secret selves are absolutely necessary. But relationships in which quadrant I grows are more helpful than relationships that do not allow for this transfer of insights. Feedback is one way of enlarging quadrant I.

Feedback, to be fruitful, needs to be as concrete as possible and to include reference to how the behavior affected you. "You are so irresponsible," "You are so dependable," "Sometimes you drive me crazy," or "I am always glad when it is your turn on duty" are not helpful. Feedback is better when it involves both reference to a particular action or issue and your response to that. It would be more helpful to say something like, "This is the third time this week you didn't return a call and that makes me angry" or "You have kept an accurate log that makes it possible for me to do the final report." Specific, concrete behavior followed by your reaction. Keep feedback brief, concise, and immediate. Never mind what happened last month; that should have been addressed last month.

I am convinced we do not give enough positive feedback to one another. Preachers report polite and superficial "That was a nice sermon" but little real, helpful feedback to their words. Professors almost never know how students feel about a course until the final impersonal and anonymous computer evaluation. When I hear students praising a professor, I always ask if they have told that professor how much they are enjoying the class. Invariably, the answer is no. They fear being seen as trying to "butter up" the teacher. Likewise, when I hear teachers praise a student's paper or report and ask the student if they have been told, very often the answer is no. One of my regular New Year's resolutions is to tell people the good things others have said about them.

Confrontation[6]

Some feedback is better discussed under the rubric of confrontation. "Confront" has the sense of sharing a common border, of meeting face-to-face.

6. *See* my "Learning to Share Our Common Border: The Role of Confrontation in Ministry," *PACE* 19 (n.d.).

It usually involves an issue that is significant to both parties, who hold different opinions. But confrontation is not necessarily just a discussion about those differences. Confrontation demands that our common border be shifted in some way, that some change be made. Ministers often have a difficult time with confrontation, growing, I believe, out of a naive expectation that the road to the reign of God will be all sweetness and light. Not so, as we can learn by reading the Acts of the Apostles. Yet confrontation is one of the vital skills a minister can learn. It is not a skill that needs to be constantly in use, but when it is needed, confrontation is sometimes a most effective ministry.

Confrontation is not just a skill, although that certainly is involved. Confrontation is a way of relating. It is, or it ought to be, communication with a person we care about. My first guideline concerning confrontation is never to confront a person for whom you do not care. Leave it to someone else. Other common sense guidelines: Be reasonable. Do not demand dramatic conversion; one behavioral change may be possible. Be immediate. Do not let things pile up and then explode. Confrontation is best when it is a conscious decision, deliberately planned and carried out. Be willing to change yourself. It may be that you don't see the whole picture or have misinterpreted a situation. That leads to one more guideline: Be tentative. Absolute pronouncements from on high are very hard to take seriously. Be descriptive. Give an account of what you see and the impact it has had on you or others. Judging, name calling, accusing, commanding, or demanding have little but negative effect on us. Why would we think they might affect others? Be specific. Clues, hints, and nonverbal messages need to be backed up with words.

When you recognize that you are reasonable, immediate, willing to change, tentative, descriptive, and specific, you still have to give some thought to the consequences of your confrontation. Confrontation is often received in the spirit in which it is done. Students sincerely want to minister as well as they are able and appreciate whatever will enable that. But students may become defensive when being asked to see a side of themselves they do not recognize. They may distort or defuse or deny the confrontation; they may ignore it. They may try to convince you that you are wrong. (And you may be!) A common defense is to agree readily with you and thus bring the conversation to a premature close. In any case, the intention is to leave it behind and do little or nothing about it. When you decide to confront, you would do well to consider possible reactions and be prepared for them.

After all that, my best advice may come as a surprise. When you can avoid confrontation, do. The great confronters of our day, Mahatma Gandhi, Martin Luther King, Jr., and Dorothy Day all avoided unnecessary confrontation and saved their energies for circumstances where they might effect some good. Confront when confrontation is the best teaching device at your disposal; otherwise look for another means to accomplish your goal. I am not suggesting a cowardly avoidance of difficult situations but rather an intelligent assessment and a careful and care-filled facing of the issue.

Evaluation[7]

Another component of supervision that makes both students and supervisors uncomfortable is evaluation. Students are constantly being evaluated: Their term papers are evaluated, their exams are evaluated, their oral reports are evaluated, their preaching is evaluated, so is their liturgical practice. Professors evaluate them, seminary staff evaluate them, they even evaluate one another. Rightly or wrongly, evaluation has a negative connotation. It suggests that someone is weighing us against a norm (that we may not agree with) and grading us on his or her perception.

Evaluation does not ordinarily have the sense of dialogue; it seems to be a one-way process. This need not be; in supervision, evaluation for the purpose of diagnosing certain attitudes or behaviors is a dialogical process. By it students can strengthen skills and avoid mistakes they may be unconscious of. Evaluation is done on the basis of some criteria—in this case, the criteria of the student's stated goals. The supervisor works with the student to reflect on a ministerial event in the light of what the student hopes to learn. Evaluation presumes that the evaluator is observant and has some (perhaps unexpressed) criteria for interpersonal and personal communication. Joanmarie Smith accents the significance of criteria by reminding us how we have been sensitized to the finer points of Olympic sports by the professional commentaries that accompany the contests. We can anticipate the score of a dive or an acrobatic feat because we have learned the criteria. An important lesson for evaluators is the difference in scores given by different judges; evaluation is never a purely objective occurrence. For the most part, students appreciate diagnostic evaluation, especially when it is carried out in a dialogic manner.

But there is another, more demanding and exacting kind of evaluation. Smith suggests that institutions of higher learning, including seminaries, exist primarily for the purpose of credentialing graduates. Conferral of a degree proclaims that the institution stands behind the graduate and guarantees

---

7. *See* Joanmarie Smith, "Evaluation: The Specifying Activity of Education," *Religious Education Journal* 79 (1984).

some minimal knowledge and skill. Moreover, we are grateful that some accredited institution has attested to the skills of our doctor, automobile mechanic, and beautician. "Our concern is that some body of objective, knowledgeable persons are willing to stake their reputation on the warranted conviction that those who provide the services we solicit do in fact have the appropriate knowledge and skills."[8] Master of Divinity programs credential men and women for ministry. They announce to the Church at large that conferral of a degree can be understood to mean the person has acquired the theory and skills for ministry. Supervisors assist in that process. Evaluation, in spite of its difficulty, must therefore be taken very seriously.

I would suggest, however, that regarding the evaluation demanded by the seminary or university, the language be changed to that of reporting. When both seminarian and supervisor are responsible to each other and to the seminary to report their perceptions of the field experience, the whole process takes on another character. Of course, the seminary wants to know how the seminarian functions in a ministerial setting, and of course the supervisor is among the best qualified to discuss that. Whatever information is sent by the supervisor, it is most advantageous to both student and seminary staff when it is a recounting of the issues involved in supervision.

The bottom line and the most important thing to be remembered is that there should never be a surprise in a final written report that is sent to the seminary. The seminary report is not the place to discuss issues that a supervisor has not already addressed with the student. The report requested by the seminary is not a final reckoning. It is meant to be a summary of the issues and concerns that have formed the supervisory conversations.

Supervisors act in cooperation with the seminary in the education of future ministers. As such, they share in the seminary's responsibility to the Church to provide the best possible ministers. Any serious question about the appropriateness of a candidate for ministry must be addressed, but the first place to address that is with the seminarian. Some supervisors are hesitant to report negative characteristics because they do not want to be responsible for "spoiling someone's opportunity" for ordination or for ministry. I would assure anyone who had such reservations that seminaries never act on only one person's perceptions; it is when the same picture is drawn by a number of people, when some pattern is detected, that serious action is taken. So many people are involved in the decision about the qualification for ministry that each is responsible for honest input, knowing that it will be supported or opposed by others.

8. Ibid., 465.

If a serious reservation exists in your mind about the advisability of the student's involvement in ministry, the sooner you discuss it with the student and the proper authorities, the better. Since education is the point, waiting until the end of the year to address problems and questions short-circuits the procedure. A secondary consideration is that the student has no way of making the necessary changes in order to pass the course. I say secondary consideration because the credits are not the most important element of any course, including the field-education course; learning is. The mention of credits suggests just how complex the relationship is. The primary focus is the ministry, the student-supervisor relationship is a significant element, and consideration must also be paid to the responsibility to the seminary (and ultimately to the Church). Besides all that, academic factors like credit do need to be attended to.

Conclusion

At the beginning of this chapter, I suggested that artists first learned the basics of their art and only then was it possible to speak of creating art. The issues raised here are meant to enliven and enspirit the novice-minister's learning. They are not arbitrarily decided-upon records. These basics of supervised field education may either be done in cursory compliance with the demands of the seminary, or they may be like colors on an artists palette or notes of a scale. Each color, each sound by itself, may be lovely, but it is only by placing the colors or the sounds together, by putting them in relationship with one another, attending to balance, texture, and intensity, that a work of art is produced. Rigid adherence to the suggestions presented here is no guarantee that the contract, case studies, and critical incidents of the student or the feedback, confrontation, and reports of the supervisor will be life producing. They, like the colors of the spectrum and notes of the scale, produce something beautiful when they are touched by the human spirit. It is akin to Corita's idea that "If you bake a cake and light the candles, something celebrative may happen."

Points for Reflection

1. For your role as supervisor write one professional goal, one project goal, and three objectives for each.

2. Consider ways to include the student's covenant/contract in your discussions through the year.

3. Read over the case presented on pages 79–80 and consider what points you would bring to a supervisory session.

4. What concrete steps could you take to include a seminarian at your place of ministry?

5. Consider how you would handle a situation in which you did not wish to support the student in ministry.

Chapter Five

Theological Reflection: Making Faith Connections

When I discussed this chapter with the students in the M. Div. program at Notre Dame, one of them said, " 'Theological Reflection' sounds somewhat academic; why not call this chapter 'Making Faith Connections'?" So be it. Theological reflection, making faith connections, helps us to recognize the "so what" behind the events of our lives. Informal theological reflection is a common occurrence. People do not always call it theological reflection, but it happens everyday. Great joy or sorrow, beautiful music, majestic mountains and quiet rivers, and certainly birth and death, are all occasions for contemplation about God's presence in our lives. News accounts of floods, famine, earthquakes, of war, crime, conflict and disease often elicit theological reflection. The search for meaning, when done in the light of faith, is theological reflection.

In the discussion with our students concerning this book, this was the chapter about which they were most concerned, the one that generated the most lively conversation. If theological reflection, trying to make sense of God's presence in our lives, is the responsibility of every Christian, why, they wanted to know, doesn't everyone know that. What they were questioning was an apparent lack of formal, structured reflection, not the fact that people regularly try to make sense of God's presence in the world in general and in their lives in particular.

Making Faith Connections

I am not talking about casual conversation about God's goodness, the dignity of human life, redemption, or the evil of sin; theological reflection in supervision is a structured conversation. Structured—not stilted, not rigid. Formal theological reflection is what *constitutes* ministerial supervision. Acquiring skills, growing as a person, developing a ministerial identity, good in themselves, might merely lead to activism. Containing crises is not the essence of ministry; faith connections need to be made. After we have given the cup of water, visited the sick, and buried the dead, with more or less pastoral expertise, we are left with the question, "So what?" How does it fit in with the scheme of things? In the words of a traditional spirituality, "What does this have to do with eternity?"

Some of us are uncomfortable with structured conversations. They seem false, studied, manipulated. But students are involved in academic pursuits and are more comfortable with structured conversations. The academic atmosphere fosters discussions about great questions, not only in the classroom, but in the dormitories, dining halls and lounges. Divinity students welcome "God-talk" and the opportunity to make the connections between the different facets of their lives.

Supervision is not just a two-way conversation about a missing third person. The supervisor and the supervisee are not alone in the process. They recognize that the Spirit is always present and waiting for an invitation to join the conversation. And that may be the precise reason why we are hesitant about the process. We know what listening to the Spirit has gotten other people into. When the disciples experienced the presence of the Spirit in the upper room, they were transformed from frightened people to charismatic preachers. They were so enthusiastic, the crowd thought they were drunk. When the Spirit is poured out, "Your sons and your daughters shall prophesy, and your young people shall see visions and your elderly shall dream dreams" (Acts 2:17). The Spirit inflames, inspires, moves us from our lethargy—no wonder we avoid the meeting whenever possible.

And that is not the only reservation. We probably agree with the novelist Joseph Heller who said "Abraham and Sarah are the only ones I know of who ever got a laugh out of a conversation with God."[1] We say "theological reflection" and think "heavy, serious, somber." But making faith connections is at times exciting, often consoling, and always challenging. It is an acknowledgement that God is intimately involved in our world but does not overstep the bounds of divine responsibility. We are still responsible. We are the ones who will bring about the reign of God. Not alone, certainly. But neither will God alone eliminate sin, suffering and evil in the world. We who profess to be ministers are involved in mystery. We minister because we are convinced that God's presence saturates our world and we have

---

1. Joseph Heller, *God Knows* (New York: Dell Books, 1984) 65.

accepted the dare to make that presence more palpable, more visible, more sensible—able to be sensed. We might liken making faith connections to putting on the kind of exotic glasses that are so common in science fiction stories—glasses that enable us to see what is invisible to the naked eye; glasses that see through material substances and around corners; glasses that make present to us what has been there all along.

Supervision that aims only at producing more efficient ministers or more successful ministry is relatively easy. It demands some effort and may succeed in its aims. But it does not help develop the kind of ministers the Church and the world so desperately need. Supervision which takes theological reflection seriously (but not soberly) is about opening both participants to change, it is about deepening the questions, not about finding answers. It involves listening to the wisdom of the saints and sinners in our past and to the wisdom of the saints and sinners in our present. Listening, not just for the purpose of hearing but in order that we may return, like the Samaritan woman at the well to the ministry renewed, transformed even. Pastoral action is a constitutive part of theological reflection. This is not knowledge for the sake of knowledge but knowledge for transformation of the self and of the world. Theological reflection, like pastoral theology, is concerned with humanity's partnership with God in renewing the face of the earth.

And because it is a human endeavor, theological reflection involves our whole being; it involves both thinking and feeling. Charlie Brown and his friends of ''Peanuts'' fame may offer a variety of approaches to theological reflection. Each year, in October, we follow the trials of Linus as he attempts to figure out ways to catch sight of the Great Pumpkin. Linus is so cerebral about the coming of the Great Pumpkin that he altogether misses the celebration of Halloween. ''We analyze, scrutinize, and categorize, and perhaps think we are doing theology when what we may actually be doing is playing intellectual games, trying to win at one-upmanship to see who has the best insight and theological acuity.''[2] Theological reflection, while it involves the intellect does not end there.

On the other end of the spectrum is Snoopy, who dances unthinkingly through life and who does not ponder the effect of his feeling-directed style. He is of course the pattern for those who ignore the intelligibility of issues and questions of systematic theology and rely solely on feelings. This too distorts human experience by excluding our rational, thinking faculties.

2. C. Roy Woodruff, ''*Theological Reflection in the Supervisory Process,*'' in *Pastoral Hermeneutics and Ministry: Theological Field Education Resources:* Volume IV edited by Donald F. Beisswenger and Doran McCarty (Association for Theological Field Education, 1983) 235. Woodruff is responsible for the ''Peanuts'' comparison.

Or we might take an absolutely certain dogmatic position on an issue. With no sense of searching for less inadequate answers to our questions we simply dig in and like Lucy, never learn, but only reinforce our own insights. Lucy has the answers, not just for her own questions, but for anyone who will listen to her. She has a claim on the truth and is therefore incapable of any real conversation.

The most reliable model for theological reflection is good old Charlie Brown. Avoiding the intellectualism of Linus, the dogmatism of Lucy, and the emotionalism of Snoopy, Charlie Brown tries to use his whole self in his struggle to seriously reflect. It is not always easy and Charlie does not always find a comforting solution. But, he does raise significant questions and in the process, risks confusion and ultimately conversion. The outcome of theological reflection is not to discover the answer to our questions but to detect deeper and more profound questions.

In spite of the fact that people engage in informal theological reflection often, I am still left with our student's query, why don't we know that theological reflection is the work of all Christians. Are Christians reticent about theological reflection because we do not have models? Because we have been accustomed to thinking that theology is bestowed from on high and all we have to do is listen and submit? This chapter will present sufficient examples, patterns and models of theological reflection so that supervisors, like good teachers, will have a repertoire from which to draw as they construct their own model. In likening this process to education, I am suggesting that it requires planning. Both the supervisor and the student have homework to do before they meet. If you have ever squirmed through a class or a homily when the teacher or minister "winged it" you know how important planning is.

The Process

In supervision, the process starts with a ministerial experience of the seminarian who is primarily responsible for deciding which issue will be discussed. This takes the form of written material presented to the supervisor at least a day in advance of the supervisory hour. Both are responsible for thinking and praying beforehand about the issue so that significant conversation is possible. It bears repeating that this is not superficial or casual conversation. When I was a very young sister, the director of novices warned us against "too much fluff and not enough stuff." Making faith connections is strong stuff, not the mouthing of pious platitudes.

Listening

The process of making faith connections demands both listening and sharing. Listening, really listening is very hard work. Listening means being fully present to the situation, attentive to signs and unexpressed clues; it means suspending premature judgment. Listening is not just hearing words. Listening to gestures, listening to the tone of voice, listening to what the eyes are saying, listening to the pauses and the silences—that is listening. I am not suggesting that you play pop psychologist but I am suggesting that you maintain a certain intensity of presence, a more than physical presence.

Listening means putting ourselves, as far as possible, in the position of speaker. Listening means being aware of feelings, attentive to body language; hearing what is said and what is left unsaid. Listening is "an ascetical exercise in self-emptying."[3] It requires that we rid ourselves of our own agenda and prejudgments in order to really hear. We only half listen if we think we already know the answer; then our interpretations shape our listening. Some people prepare their responses as others speak. They wait until the speaker takes a breath and jump in with their own remarks. They haven't really been listening.

Listening also involves the skill of questioning. And one of the most significant questions may be "Is this what you are saying?" It not only helps the supervisor to be clear about what the student is saying, it gives the student the chance to restate the particular theological stance, to articulate more lucidly what is meant. The discussion ought not be a question and answer contest but questioning is a significant element in the listening process. Since the purpose of the reflection is to help the students make sense of their own theology of ministry, it is important that they have the opportunity to articulate that theology. In verbalizing their theological convictions, students are able to bring their professed theology and operative theology more in line with one another. As they speak, they begin to see where the consistencies and inconsistencies are.

Listening to the student is only the beginning. Supervisors must also keep their ears attuned to the contributions of the Christian Tradition and of the culture. Listening to the Spirit present in all facets of life is the essence of theological reflection.

Sharing

Attentive listening is only one half of the conversation; it is essential that the supervisor share her or his own faith. Sharing takes seriously the responsi-

3. Whitehead Ibid., 87.

bility of each partner to contribute to the conversation. Supervisors have a significant contribution to make in confessing their theological convictions. This requires both humility and courage. Stating unfinished thoughts, exchanging half-formed ideas, admitting one's uncertainties, standing up for one's values and beliefs in the face of alternative views is not easy. But since we are asking the students to do it, it is only right that we assume the same responsibility.

Articulating our own beliefs and visions is only part of sharing; feedback and challenging are also part of the package.[4] Challenge is an important part of deepening a belief, it requires us to clear up fuzzy thinking, to find just the right words to communicate our meaning, to see something we had not seen before. We cannot uncritically accept the thoughts and feelings of the student. We cannot count their experience as the measure of truth. We cannot leave their considerations unexamined. A critical balance of affirmation and challenge broadens the seminarian's understanding of her or him self and of ministry. The supervisory relationship is one place where students may become aware of how other people perceive them. The supervisor who affirms and supports a seminarian at appropriate times can more easily be heard by the student when challenging is more suitable. Supervision is not confession of faults but it is the place where a student can become aware of areas in which growth is necessary.

Groome's Model

The models I discussed in chapter three under the heading of education are equally rich as models for theological reflection. None of them simply impose the teachings of bishops, theologians, or other experts upon experience. In each, the conversation brings Scripture, tradition, experience and culture, into play and the critique and challenge goes both ways. Religiously significant information is gleaned from all the sources of God's revelation. Tom Groome strives to knit together individual stories and the Christian story. If this method is agreed upon by both student and supervisor, the preparation for the discussion might find each searching the Scriptures, or the lives of the saints (living and dead), or the teachings of theologians and the hierarchy (living or dead) to find the connections between our tradition and the present concern. This may be a good place to say that the connections ought not be strained or artificial. If we force a relationship, it will unravel rather than knit together. When that seems to be happening, the best thing is to

---

4. See chapter four, pages 82–84.

admit that the connections seem too tenuous. Instead, what may need to be discussed is why are we having a hard time seeing how this relates to God?

The Whitehead's Model

In Evelyn and Jim Whitehead's tripolar model, culture is invited into the conversation between experience and tradition. We sometimes lose sight of God when we only look in so-called sacred places. Philosophy, psychology, sociology, political interpretations and the wisdom of other religious traditions are some of "the diverse ways that God speaks to us from the broader culture which lies beyond our own limited experience and the historically specific tradition of Christianity."[5] Art is another powerful communicator of God's presence.

Artists are usually twenty or thirty years ahead of theologians in being able to articulate the theology of a culture. They seem especially gifted in opening our eyes to the presence of transcendence. Picasso's "Guernica," Lorraine Hansberry's "Raisin in the Sun," Carlos Fuentes' *The Good Conscience* preceded Church statements on war, racism and the tension between personal sin and systemic evil by more than a generation.

Lily Tomlin is an acute "cultural theologian." As Trudy, the bag lady, she converses regularly with creatures from outer space. Much of her conversation with them has profound religious and ethical impact. For instance, Trudy tries to help them to understand the difference between soup and art by repeatedly showing them a can of soup and an Andy Warhol painting. "Soup . . . art . . ." as she hides one or the other behind her back. At the end of the play, when Trudy and her friends sneak into a theater, she realizes that they have goosebumps (another concept they could not understand). Then Trudy remembers that she had forgotten to tell them to watch the play, they had been watching the audience, strangers sitting in the dark, laughing and crying about the same thing. They said, "Trudy, the play was soup, the audience . . . art." Trudy ends the play with:

> I like to think of them out there in the dark, watching us. Sometimes, we'll do something and they'll laugh. Sometimes, we'll do something and they'll cry. And maybe one day we'll do something so magnificent, everyone in the universe will get goosebumps.[6]

Can Trudy be pointing to the coming reign of God when all of creation will get goosebumps seeing how we are enabling the coming of the reign

5. Whitehead, *Method in Ministry*, 20.

6. Jane Wagner, *The Search for Signs of Intelligent Life in the Universe.* (New York: Harper and Row, 1986).

of justice, peace and love? Certainly she clues us to the fact that there are times when theological reflection is not explicitly "God talk."

Significant religious truths are sometimes hidden in other metaphors and symbols. The practice of making faith connections sensitizes us to those metaphors and symbols and reveals their truth. Marilyn French, in writing about Tomlin's one woman show, says that "the audience keeps clapping, clapping, sending a message, telling [Tomlin], telling each other, that they have that night received the gift of truth."[7]

Holland and Henriot's Model

Joe Holland and Peter Henriot are more explicit about bringing social analysis and theological reflection together into one coherent piece. Their pattern is particularly helpful when it is necessary to make connections between individual sin and systemic sin. While Groome's model might be most helpful when the focus is on the student minister, Holland and Henriot's is when the focus in on the ministerial situation. In any case, the process would be short circuited if the faith connections were not made. Theological reflection is not like icing on a cake, something that improves the taste and looks nice; it is more like the flour, eggs and shortening, without which the cake would not be.

To reiterate, theological reflection is not an intellectual exercise for the sheer delight of playing with interesting ideas. Its aim is not only religious insight but insightful religious action. The minister is not a philosopher or theologian who may put off decisions until all the data is in. The minister has to make pastoral decisions in the here and now, often with incomplete information. Our responsibility is to avoid uninformed decisions, to arrive at less inadequate conclusions. Supervision is concerned with the present and future ministry of the student. Students are constantly in the process of making decisions about their ministerial style, about acquiring skills and strategies, about alternative ways of handling situations, about causes and connections. The action called for does not always mean taking some public stand or providing new services. It may be that the action will be to pray, to turn the problem over to someone else, to continue in an already established way. Whatever the decision, the ministry will be richer than a response to people's needs which is unreflective.

Models and theories about theological reflection, while helpful in themselves, are enriched by narrative. Stories, parables, illustrations fill out the

---

7. Afterword, *The Search for Intelligent Life in the Universe*, 223.

picture. I will present examples of theological reflection from student's experience, from literature and from Scripture so that what has been suggested by way of theory may become incarnate in the story.

Theological Reflection in Ministry

In preparing for a supervisory session, students present a written report of a ministerial event as discussed in chapter four. The journal entry may be in the form of a critical incident, a case study, a verbatim. It must be remembered that what is presented for reflection is the student's reading of the situation; someone else may give a whole different perspective on what happened. In spite of that, the journal does represent the memory and understanding that the seminarian has of the reported incident. It is that understanding which provides the basis for theological reflection. It may not be the truth, the whole truth and nothing but the truth, but it still does reveal enough about the student for reflection.

Students come with their own questions which may begin the supervisory conversation and it is well to address those issues first, but the supervisor also raises issues which the student may have missed. Each supervisor will bring different instincts and insights to the process. There is no one right way. In order to illustrate that point, I have asked a few supervisors to respond to the following issues raised by students; to suggest what they might bring to the theological reflection.

Rosa's Case Study:

Judy, a twenty-year-old college junior is an active church volunteer. She comes from a conservative family and sometimes seems to be overly dependent, to lack initiative. I find myself impatient with her at times.

Verbatim:

J:1 I need to talk to you, it's really important, do you have time now?

R:1 Sure, Judy, is something wrong?

J:2 Not really, I'm just confused. I didn't sign up to be a Bible Studies Discussion Leader.

R:2 I noticed that.

J:3 I couldn't bring myself to go to the meeting. I guess it's because I feel unworthy.

R:3 Unworthy? I don't understand that. How do you feel unworthy?

J:4 Well, my relationship with God is not what it should be. I haven't gone to church in a couple of months. And I don't pray often either.

R:4 How do you mean you don't pray well?

J:5 I don't feel good when I pray like I used to . . . I wonder if God is out there. . . . I don't think anyone is listening.

R:5 Let's talk about that. Where is God for you?

J:6 Well, I think that God is out there listening to everyone's prayers. But I really don't feel Him except when I get a warm sort of feeling when I pray. Lately, I don't feel that and I'm scared. Suppose He isn't out there. Then I am guilty thinking like this.

R:6 It sounds like you are going through a "dry period" in your relationship with God. Do you ever have those times with your friends? I think sometimes we have the same experience with God.

J:7 How do I deal with it, though? I don't even feel like I should think that God might not be there.

We then shared our ideas about God and prayer. We talked about how we felt the presence of God and what "going to church" meant in our relationship with God. We also talked about doubt and how it may have a place in prayer. I spoke from my own experience and tried to help Judy do the same. We agreed to meet again in about a week.

Interpersonal Analysis: I caught myself thinking "you" statements when I was talking and had to catch myself and change them to "I" statements.

I tried to help Judy listen to her own theology so that she could gain some perspective on her relationship with God without trying to compare how she thinks it ought to be.

Theological Analysis: As I was writing this in my journal, I realized that I had articulated a sacramental theology. We talked a great deal about "presence" and I found that Judy's ideas were very different from mine. It seemed that sacramental model met institutional model.

Supervisors' Responses: When I asked supervisors what they would focus on in this situation, one supervisor responded, "I would ask Rosa to look at her close connection between 'conservative, lack of initiative and impatient' in the beginning of her presentation and her distancing herself from the institution at the end of the case. The institution is there and it may be a source of frustration, especially for women, but it can not be dismissed. Some questions I might raise are: 'How do you feel about the institutional Church? How will you minister in an institutional setting?' I would try to get Rosa to spell out what she means by her sacramental model. How would ministry look? Community? I would share my own model which is more in the servant mode."

Another supervisor took a different approach. "I would begin where she left off.

J:7 asks 'How do you deal with it (God's absence)?' How do you?"

I would ask the students "How do you?"

Sometimes students present journal entries for discussion with their supervisors that are musings on ministry rather than straight-forward reports of an incident in ministry. One seminarian, in reflecting on his tendency to adjust to each situation, wrote, "One insight into my theology of ministry has been a growing awareness of my tendency to adopt varying tactics depending on the situation at hand. In general, before I 'enter the fray' I try to understand what is going on, and I make an assessment about what needs to be done based on what is going on. This means that I can take several different roles, and I think I have done that both in team meetings and in ministry: animator of conversation or interchange, 'herald,' summarizer, patient observer. This being said, I think that I generally prefer to have an active role, and find myself speaking often. I have also been affirmed because some of the team members have spoken with me personally in more private matters."

In responding to this entry, one supervisor suggested that he would begin with a few minutes of silence while he and the seminarian thought about instances where Jesus acted differently in various situations. His question then would be, "What do the several faces of Jesus tell about ministry? What was constant in each of the situations? What remains constant even as you change in different situations?" His questions centered on the motivation for changing according to the circumstance. He felt it would be important to have the seminarian also reflect on what he was not willing to adjust to.

Theological Reflection in Literature

Some authors produce works that make faith connections from the first chapter to the last. Their language is not always theological, but the message is clearly religious. Writers know that dialogues can teach better than pronouncements; narratives touch more deeply than dogmas.

The Trial of God

Nobel prize winner Elie Weisel, with insights born of the Holocaust, introduces characters (young and old, male and female, Jew and Gentile) who engage in profound theological reflection. In "The Trial of God," a play set in an inn of the seventeenth century, God is accused in a court of justice. The charge is that God was unfaithful to the covenant by allowing almost a whole town to be destroyed in a pogrom. It is Purim, a joyous feast with games and masks and visitors have come to the inn. The innkeeper, Berish, one of only two survivors of the massacre, acts as prosecutor but no one can be found to serve as defense council for God. Finally a stranger who identifies himself only as Sam agrees to take on the job.

Sam defends God with, ". . . why evil—why ugliness? If God chooses not to answer, He must have His reasons. God is God . . . . Endure, accept. And say Amen." But Berish replies, "Never! If He wants my life, let Him take it. . . . How can you speak of grace and charity after a pogrom?" Sam: "Is there no more propitious time to speak about them? You are alive— isn't that proof of His Kindness?" . . . . Berish: "What if I told you that He spared me not out of kindness but out of cruelty?"[8]

Another attack is imminent. Berish is offered a way out. But when a priest urges him to feign acceptance of the cross, he refuses. Sam, thinking he has won, cries that Berish opted for God and against the enemies of God. But Berish insists, "I have not opted for God. I'm against His enemies, that's all." Sam piously responds, "I'm His servant. He created the world and me without asking for my opinion; He may do with both whatever He wishes. Our task is to glorify Him, to praise Him, to love Him—in spite of our- selves."[9] The guests wonder if Sam is a saintly rabbi, a miracle-maker, a mys- tical dreamer on his way to meet—and help them meet—the Redeemer.

It is only when Sam puts on a fiendish Purim mask that he is recognized as Satan.

My point in including "The Trial of God," is not to suggest that even the devil does theological reflection, but only to propose that the process is not echoing pious platitudes, repeating devout phrases. The purpose of theo- logical reflection is not to defend God in the face of overwhelming evil and suffering but to come to grips with demanding questions as honestly as we can. And that sometimes includes anger—even against God. Weisel contends that his inspiration for the story came from three rabbis who "in the king- dom of night," that was the concentration camp, decided to indict God for the Holocaust. They found God guilty and then, the trial over, one of them reminded the others that the hour of prayer had arrived. And they bowed their heads and prayed.

Timidity in theological reflection sometimes prevents the breakthrough to a more profound relationship with God. Like Jacob (Gen 32) we are some- times called to wrestle with God. And like Jacob we may come out limping but with a new identity. For it was in the wrestling that Jacob became Israel— "the one who contends with God."

Moses to Her People

The music composed and sung by Harriet Tubman and others like her who became liberators of their people are clear examples of the power of bring-

8. Elie Weisel, *The Trial of God (As It Was Held on February 25, 1649 in Shamgord)* (New York: Random House, 1979) 132–133.
9. Ibid., 157.

ing present experience and faith in dialogue. The Moses of her people helped them to see their slavery through the metaphor of the Exodus. And once slavery was seen through the lens of Scripture, decisive action was demanded, even of the terrified. When she sang, they came to new understandings of their slavery and of what was now being demanded of them by Tubman and by God.

> When Israel was in Egypt Land,
> Let my people go.
> Oppressed so hard they could not stand.
> Let my people go.
> Go down, Moses, way down in Egypt's Land,
> Tell old Pharaoh,
> Let my people go.

Once the slaves paralleled their lives with the Exodus, the linkage made the perilous road to freedom urgent. Theological reflection is concerned with understanding our lives through the symbols of Christianity. They provide a lens through which the experience is redeemed—not glossed over, not denied, not necessarily bettered but always challenging to action. Theological reflection is not about learning how to manipulate God but how to respond to God's inspiration.

Shug and Celie

Theological reflection is not always focused directly on the great systemic evils like the Holocaust or slavery. Often the relationship with God is spoken of in more personal ways. Alice Walker's *The Color Purple* is chock full of theological insights but especially in one conversation between Shug and Celie.

Celie records: "All my life I never care what people thought bout nothing I did, I say. But deep in my heart I care about God. What he going to think. And come to find out, he don't think. Just sit up there glorying in being deef, I reckon. But it ain't easy, trying to do without God. Even if you know he ain't there, trying to do without him is a strain." After Shug admits to being a sinner, she says, "Us worry bout God a lot. But once us feel loved by God, us do the best us can to please him with what us like." "You telling me God love you, and you ain't never done nothing for him? I mean, not go to church, sing in the choir, feed the preacher and all like that?"

"But if God love me, Celie, I don't have to do all that. . . . I can lay back and just admire stuff. Be happy. Have a good time." Well this sounds like blasphemy sure nuff.

She say, "Celie, tell the truth, have you ever found God in Church? I never did. I just found a bunch of folks hoping for him to show. Any God I ever felt in church I brought in with me. And I think all the other folks did too. They come to church to share God, not find God."[10]

Theological Reflection in Scripture

Scripture teaches more by stories than by abstract theories. Stories and parables convey meaning on many levels. In the telling and retelling, stories and parables are kept alive and grow and develop new meanings with each listening. Let us look at some Gospel stories for hints about theological reflection. In each case, the pattern is similar: the discussion begins with present experience, that experience is itself reflected upon and the faith tradition is introduced into conversation. The process leaves the participants changed and called to some new action.

The Woman at the Well

The conversation between the Samaritan woman and Jesus begins with a request for water, a simple enough request in an arid setting. The unnamed woman recognizes him as a Jew and reflects on the division between the Jews and her people, the enmity between them. She may be wondering about Jesus drinking from a cup that Jews would call unclean. Jesus moves the conversation from well water to living water. In the light of her theological awareness evident in the subsequent discussion, it is likely that she understands his meaning. She asks for the living water, a common enough symbol for revelation, wisdom, divine life; even the Torah was described as living water. This woman knows her theology; the conversation, from beginning to end has to do with religious issues—even the discussion of the five "baals," (usually translated husbands and leading to the perception of her as a sinner).[11]

"Baal" may be translated "Lord, Master, Husband, God." Let us suppose that Jesus tells her to call her own god for living water. She replies that she has no god, and Jesus agrees the Samaritans had strayed from the worship of the one true God when they brought the five pagan gods back from captivity with them.[12] It is at this point in their theological reflection that

10. Alice Walker, *The Color Purple* (New York: Harcourt, Brace, Jovanovich, 1982) 175–177.
11. I try to restore this Samaritan woman's good reputation whenever I can. Because she was labelled sinner (sexually loose), I was blind for a long time to the fact that she was respected enough in her community that her neighbors would listen to her and follow her to Jesus.
12. 2 Kings 17:29-41 records the history of the Samaritan's obstinacy regarding their pagan

a new insight is opened to her. She recognizes Jesus as a prophet—the only role of the prophet being to call sinners back to the worship of the one true God.

The woman introduces the question of where to pray and receives that beautiful reply that "the hour is coming and now is, when the true worshipers will worship the Father in spirit and in truth" [John 4:23]. Then she speaks of the Messiah and receives an even greater revelation: "I who speak to you am he." As a result of the conversation, she is called to ministry. She leaves her water jar, even as Peter and the others left their boats, their nets and their fathers' house. She returns to her town and "Many Samaritans from the town believed in him because of the woman's testimony" [John 4:39]. On the strength of her word, her neighbors recognize Jesus as the Savior of the world. It seems unlikely that the town "loose" woman would have had that kind of influence.

Her understanding of Jesus in the process deepened from Jew to Prophet, to Messiah, to Savior of the world. Theological reflection gives deeper meaning to our faith; it also impels us to action because of that renewed faith. The woman returned to her town a changed woman, on fire with the good news, with a message for her people that would change them too forever.

The Syrophoenician Woman

In this story it is Jesus who is moved to change and to action. The story of the Syrophoenician woman begins, as do all theological reflections, with her present experience. Her daughter is sick, possessed by an unclean spirit. She begins the conversation by describing the daughter's illness. Jesus, in what sounds like a rather cold rebuff reminds her that the Jews (the children), must be fed first, it is not right to take the bread of the children and throw it to the dogs. "This saying ascribed to Jesus, then, argues that the gospel of the basileia . . . should not be given to Gentiles for fear they might misuse it. . . . The argument . . . is countered by the woman by referring to the messianic abundance of Christian table community. The gracious goodness of the God of Jesus is abundant enough to satisfy Jews but also the Gen-

gods. Men of Babylon, Cuth, and Hameth, the Avvites and Sepharvites returned from captivity with the gods from each place. (Five places of exile are mentioned.) "To this day they do according to the former manner;" . . . "they did according to their former manner" and "So these nations feared the Lord and also served their graven images; their children likewise and their children's children—as their fathers did, so they do to this day."

This understanding that they were talking about gods and not husbands makes sense in the light of the tenor of the whole conversation and also in the light of Jesus's lack of attention to "sexual sins."

tiles.''[13] She knows he is speaking from the perspective of his Jewish culture and tradition but her insights help him to expand his understanding of his mission.

This is a powerful example of the benefit of really listening to others even when their saying is hard. Jesus certainly sounds firm in his belief about the primacy of Israel but because she can hear his words as the understanding of a faithful Jew, she is able to challenge those words in such a way that he can hear her. And because he hears her interpretation, he can understand that his mission extends beyond Israel. "Her wit, her sharp retort, was indeed her gift to Jesus—gift that enabled his gift of healing in turn, her ministry that opened up the possibility of his . . . . There appears to be a theological point: It sets forth who Jesus is as the Christ of God.''[14] Jesus learns from a poor outcast a new vision of his mission. Theological reflection is not a game of finding enough arguments to shore up our own beliefs and ideas in order to win an argument; it is more often about the stretching of those beliefs and ideas. It says we don't yet have all the answers and may have to change our minds. Even Jesus did.

The Disciples on the Road to Emmaus

Two disciples are on the road from Jerusalem to their home in Emmaus after Jesus has been crucified. As a stranger joins them, the discussion begins, as always, not with theory but with their present reality. They have just witnessed the death of Jesus and with it the death of all their dreams. When the risen Lord joins them, they do not recognize him immediately. (Theological reflection doesn't offer premature insights.) But when Jesus puts their experience in conversation with the Scriptures, they begin to understand. Theological reflection enables them to redefine their loss and the suffering and death of Jesus in the light of the word of God. At the table, their eyes are opened, they recognize Jesus and they have to return from whence they came. Their call is to return to the community and share the resurrection experience they had had.

Each of these examples presents a guide of sorts for theological reflection. Begin with experience, bring the tradition into conversation with that experience, leave room for surprise, and be ready to leave our water jug, or

---

13. Elisabeth Schüssler Fiorenza, *In Memory of Her: A Feminist Theological Reconstruction of Christian Origins* (New York: Crossroad, 1983) 137–138.

14. Sharon H. Ringe, "A Gentile Woman's Story" in *Feminist Interpretation of the Bible* edited by Letty M. Russell (Philadelphia: Westminster, 1985) 71–72.

accept a new understanding or simply return to the place we have just left to share our good news and hear the good news the community has to offer.

These musings from Scripture do not offer a sure-proof method. They are rather, "feeling our way along from moment to moment in uncharted territory, meeting the next unknown moment with a sense of wonder and trust in the shared exploration."[15] Expect surprises—"I am He." "Even the dogs eat the crumbs." "Their eyes were opened and they recognized Him."

Some Topics for Exploration in Supervision

In the examples of theological reflection, I tried to choose a variety of styles so that you would realize that everything may be grist for the mill. If we really believe that God is everywhere, that God is the Ground of our very being, that God is involved in human endeavors, then we can use any human experience for theological reflection. There are, however, a few issues which I think are so universal that they bear special attention when working with student ministers. The first of these is the Messiah complex.[16] Idealistic and inexperienced people are especially prone to dreams of saving the whole world; in the process, they often arrive at solutions precipitously, wear out prematurely and suffer unnecessary discouragement.

"Messiahs" are helpaholics who attempt to earn a sense of worth by acting worthily. They often allow the needs, wishes and demands of others to determine their actions and depend on the gratitude of those they help to feel good about themselves. Messiahs work twenty-five hours a day; they are praised for their dedication and availability; they are often too busy to develop intimate relationships. Carmen Renee Berry lists seven styles messiahs tend to take: 1) Pleasers who feel responsible for other people's happiness; 2) Rescuers who are always on call, bounce from crisis to crisis, trauma to trauma; 3) Givers to whom the opportunity to give is viewed as an obligation and who are unable to place realistic limits on giving; 4) Counselors who take on the worries and problems of others while avoiding facing their own; 5) Protectors who take the responsibility for making choices for others; and try to save people from themselves; 6) Teachers for whom the desire to communicate "their message" with a group becomes an obligation rather than

---

15. Stephen Levine, *Meeting at the Edge: Dialogues With the Grieving and the Dying* (New York: Doubleday, 1984) xi.

16. See Carmen Renee Berry, *When Helping You is Hurting Me* (San Francisco: Harper and Row, 1988) and Evelyn Eaton Whitehead and James D. Whitehead, *Method in Ministry*, chapter 10, "A Christian Ascetism of Time."

a choice; and finally, 7) Crusaders with an acute sense of justice that demands that the world change yesterday.[17]

Of course, every one of the messiah types may be healthy ministerial styles. They become destructive when ministers become overextended and over-invested in the lives of the persons they are trying to assist. Reflecting on a theology of ministry, on motivation for ministry may help to discover the difference and foster a healthy and holy commitment to ministry. "Rather than imitating the hectic, overly busy and distracted lifestyle so common in American society today, ascetical Christians might be expected to give their work time a different quality. Someone who believes that our work and careers belong to a larger process of change and redemption, that we are not solely responsible for the future of the world, needs to be less frenetic and compul-sive. Such a person can afford to be friendlier with time, and witness to a style of living both more relaxed and more aware."[18]

When I speak of the Messiah complex, the students tease me by parrot-ing back, "Care for the caregiver." One seminarian asked if I thought that Dorothy Day, Bishop Desmond Tutu or Oscar Romero cared for the caregiver. "Yes, yes, and yes." Care for the caregiver does not mean exotic vacations or frequent days at the golf course; it doesn't mean a narcissistic preoccupa-tion with oneself. It does mean considering one's own physical, spiritual and emotional health; it means nurturing relationships; it means attending to who we are as well as what we do.

A second rather universal topic for theological reflection is collaborative ministry.[19] The age of kindly old Father Flynn caring for the flock and mak-ing all the decisions himself is over. (If not entirely over, it certainly is dy-ing.) Today's seminarians must learn to minister with other Christians, who may be more talented in some areas, more experienced in others and who expect their contributions to be taken seriously. At the same time, there are few models of collaborative ministry for students to study, few examples of Christian communities who truly cooperate in their efforts to live out the Gospel mandate.

In regard to collaborative ministry, it seems that many parishes and agen-cies are caught somewhere between stages II and III described by Loughlan

17. Ibid., 41–55.
18. Whitehead, *Method in Ministry*, 161.
19. See, for instance William Bausch, *The Hands-On Parish* (Mystic, Connecticut, 1989); Dody Donnelly, C.S.J., *Team: Theory and Practice of Team Ministry* (New York: Paulist Press, 1979); James D. Whitehead and Evelyn Eaton Whitehead, *The Emerging Laity: Returning Leader-ship to the Community of Faith* (Garden City, NY: Doubleday, 1986); Letty Russell, *The Fu-ture of Partnership* (Philadelphia: Westminster: 1979) and *Growth in Partnership* (Philadelphia: Westminster, 1981).

Sofield and Carroll Juliano.[20] Having moved beyond the hierarchical model (stage I) in which collaboration was not a value, many are obsessed with talking about collaboration (stage II), but are unable to move through their ambivalence and fear about what collaboration will cost (stage III). Very few appear to have finally committed themselves to collaboration as the mode of ministry (stage IV). Yet in many other facets of life, women and men are learning to live and work together in a more cooperative way. Women and men who are preparing themselves to minister in the church of the future have grown up in a society that values, at least in theory, cooperation and teamwork. They need all the help we can give them to be able to translate those values into their reflections about ministering together. They need the skills, theory and motivation to be able to minister in a church that recognizes and fosters the gifts of the community and each one in the community. For some, it may mean learning to become dependent on others, relinquishing the thought of being "in charge;" for others, it may mean learning to be independent, assuming responsibilities once assumed by authority figures. For both it means learning to be interdependent, a situation that is not possible without both dependence and independence.

Conclusion

You will probably think of other topics for theological reflection, topics that arise out of your own experience and concern for the church. No matter what the subject, the important thing is to help the seminarian to make faith connections, to search for meaning, to ask "So what?" How does faith in Jesus and his message affect each situation? Theological reflection *constitutes* supervision, it is not an extra added attraction that may be ignored. It is the very heart of the supervisory relationship.

As I have already suggested, our work is not to make God present, but to be aware that God permeates our world, that God may be found in the midst of suffering and in the midst of joy. In the process of reflection, we open ourselves to the ever present Spirit with the expectation that we shall be as the disciples were on the first Pentecost. When the Spirit is poured out, our sons and our daughters shall prophesy, and our young people shall see visions and our elderly shall dream dreams. The Spirit will inflame, inspire, and give us the strength to renew the face of the earth. Theological reflection enables us to return to the ministry with deeper faith, more ardent zeal and gentler compassion. We can give no greater gift to the Church and

20. *Collaborative Ministry*, 18–19.

the world than to help in the transformation and education of disciples faithful, zealous and compassionate.

Points for Reflection

1. Why is theological reflection so difficult for some people?
2. Can you think of other examples of theological reflection in Scripture or literature?
3. What issues would you raise with the students in the cases recorded here?
4. Does the Messiah complex describe your ministry? If your answer is yes, how will that influence supervision?
5. Is your ministerial setting a good example of collaborative ministry? If not, what is the seminarian learning about ministry?

Appendix

The Program of Priestly Formation
Third Edition, November 30, 1981
National Conference of Catholic Bishops, U.S.A.

Chapter Four: Pastoral Formation

Article Two: Field Education Program

195. This section, however, is not concerned with the academic curriculum as such. Rather it proposes a field education program that is to be coordinated with and integrated into the academic sphere. This program aims to provide the seminarians with an opportunity for personal involvement in and practical exercise of the pastoral ministry. This is in accordance with the recognition by the Fathers of the Second Vatican Council that seminarians need to "learn the art of exercising the apostolate not only in theory but in practice. . . ." (Decree on the Training of Priests, no. 30).

196. The custom of engaging in apostolic works is common in seminaries today, but the essential role that this should play in the total educational and formative process has recently been recognized in a fuller way. This dimension of learning through active engagement in the ministry must be seen as an integral part of the total formation of the future priest, drawing from the academic and spiritual aspects and, in turn, feeding back into and enriching them. Active pastoral involvement, if carefully designed and properly supervised—an absolute necessity—is just as educational in nature as is classroom work. The latter provides the necessary theoretical background for the priests on mission, the former is a laboratory for learning through practice.

Article Three: Objectives of the Field Education Program

197. One of the principle goals of a field education program is to teach the seminarians the habit of theological reflection about priestly mission. In the context of field education, theological reflection refers to that process by which they attempt to perceive how theology and the tradition of the Church shed light on various pastoral

111

situations they have experienced, how God's saving power and presence are operative in these experiences, and what this meant for their own life in Christ. Theological reflection is then an attempt to identify God's saving power and presence in the events of the daily lives of all people, in order to understand more clearly the mystery of life and grace and the demands of God upon themselves and the Church. Moreover, as the seminarians engage in their active apostolate, they will be forced again and again to consider how their pastoral activity fulfills the mandate of Christ, how the various forms of the apostolate establish and build up the Church among men and women, how the needs of the People of God are being met by their service and witness. As they do this, under the direction of supervisors with pastoral experience and theological competence, their academic work and the apostolate will reinforce one another, and they will recognize the theological disciplines as relevant to their mission. Working side by side with priests and other ministers who show forth the spirit of Christ will not only inspire the seminarians, but will also capitalize on the process of learning by example and identification, an aspect of education that has been profitably used in medicine and other professions, but seldom used in theological education. Thus the field education program can be the best integrating force in the total formation process, manifesting and increasing the relevance of theology and linking more closely the apostolic and spiritual aspects of the students' lives.

198. It is also important for other reasons that the seminarians be introduced into the apostolate during their time of preparation for the priesthood. The preservation and fostering of their zeal, the nourishing of their calling to the priesthood, not to speak of the vocation they share with all baptized Christians, all demand that they be engaged, at least to some degree, in the vineyard of the Lord. Thus will they be cooperating in a real salvific work, but in such circumstances and under such conditions that their apostolic work also becomes a truly educational experience. Their decision on whether or not they should move ahead to the priesthood will be put to a realistic test, as they see more clearly what a priest's life will demand of them. They will undergo the maturing experience of frustration that is a part of life and of the following of Christ. Thus they will be able to develop the responsibility, initiative, and obedience that the priestly life demands. They will also experience working within the structure of the Church, where there is a hierarchy of mission and authority. At the same time, those charged with judging the students' fitness will have the great advantage of seeing them under conditions which will more clearly approximate their future life as priests. Their judgement will be all the more sound and more confident. They will be able to answer with a greater degree of assurance than ever before the question, "What kind of priest will this seminarian be?"

199. Priests, perhaps more today than at any time in the Church's history must develop a fine sensitivity to people, their needs and aspirations, their circumstance of life, their attitudes toward God and humankind. Only if the seminarians develop this sensitivity and awareness will they be able to enter fruitfully into that "dialogue amongst men" which the "Decree on the Training of Priests" urges on them (no. 19). A prime result of a good field education program is precisely the fostering of

this dialogue, with the added benefit that such dialogue is continually seen not as a merely human endeavor but as part of the work of salvation. In addition, the seminarians will ". . . be carefully taught how to inspire and encourage apostolic action among the laity" (no. 20), and be led to an appreciation of what the global mission of the Church is, so that they are ready to ". . . meet the needs of the whole Church, being prepared in spirit to preach the Gospel everywhere" (no. 20).

Article Four: Field Education as a Stimulating and Integrating Force

200. The experience of pastoral service, combined with responsible supervision and theological reflection, should be an important stimulus for the spiritual, personal and academic development of the seminarians, as well as an integrating force in their lives. This last point is especially important, since one of the greatest needs of the seminarians is to integrate all the factors involved in their growth—spiritual, emotional, physical and academic. Challenged by the pastoral demands of their work with people of various degrees of belief, the seminarian will be forced to theological reflection, to personal profession of faith, and to deeper academic exploration.

201. With regard to their spiritual development, the seminarians' vision of faith and of God's work in people's lives will no longer be restricted to their fellow seminarians and to the seminary community; it will include a close observation of the men, women, and children they are serving in their apostolic work, and it should extend to all peoples, for whom they should show a great interest and nurture a deep concern.

202. Increased humility should be the first result as they see lives different from their own, lives which call for different responses to God and different virtues to be emphasized. Their humility will thus involve a readiness to listen and to learn, but they will also observe people's need for the Lord, and will rejoice and give thanks, seeing God's work in them. Recognizing how their own efforts can be of help and how comfortable and easy they must be in speaking about God and in reflecting confidence in God, they should be more convinced of their need to grow continuously in union with the redeeming Lord and to reflect in prayer that it is "God who gives the growth" (1 Cor 3:7).

203. A field education program will help the seminarians achieve a greater degree of personal and emotional maturity and grow in a sense of reality; it will force them to accept new responsibilities, while relinquishing others. Experience has shown that students are forced to resolve some of the personal crises that inevitably arise from contact with the needs of others. Moreover, this pastoral experience will also make the students aware of the tensions that will exist in their lives as priests, especially the tensions brought about by the need to serve, to pray, and to study. Of necessity, they will begin to search for a way to balance these tensions and to call upon such resources as spiritual direction and counseling to deal with them.

204. As a result of their pastoral experiences and theological reflection upon them, the students should begin to grasp more clearly the significance of what they have

learned in the classroom and this should help them to come to terms even more with the meaning of their faith. The students' pastoral experiences should also make them realize how much they do not know, and perhaps can never know, about the mystery of God's activity in the world. This in turn should make them more open to further study and thought about the mystery of God as well as to the hand of God in their own lives and in the lives of others. Finally, this pastoral experience will provide the students with more concrete questions with which to approach their theological studies.

205. All of this does not mean that the seminarians at the end of their formal period of education will be men who have reached their full growth, either emotionally or intellectually, either in theological experience or in pastoral experience. But a program that carefully balances and integrates the academic, spiritual and apostolic aspects of the formative process will produce priests who are capable of assuming the burdens of the pastoral ministry and ready to continue, in an independent way, the multifaceted growth process well begun in the seminary.

Handbook for Supervisors

Master of Divinity
Program
University of Notre Dame

General Expectations of the Supervision Component
of the Field Education Sequence

The student will provide the supervisor a copy of the Field Education contract. This document lists the student's goals and responsibilities in the ministerial placement site. It also specifies the dates and times the student will be at the site according to the University calendar, excluding breaks and vacations.

Supervisory sessions are to be scheduled on a regular basis. The general expectation is that the first year student will meet with the supervisor every week for a minimum of 30 minutes. Should supervisor prefer, the sessions may be scheduled for an hour every other week for the second and third year students.

The student and supervisor should agree on the kind of advance preparation the student will undertake for each supervisory session. Notre Dame students are familiar with the personal journal, verbatim, case study, pastoral log, and phenomenologizing as methods of recording their pastoral experiences. A student can be asked to make use of any of these methods. The supervisor or the student may suggest other methods of making the student's experiences or questions available to the supervisory session. It is necessary and expected that the student provide this journal entry to the supervisor at least 24 hours in advance of the supervisory session itself, in order that the supervisor may review it in preparation for the session.

At the end of each semester the student will prepare for the Field Education staff a written evaluation of the Field Education experience. These evaluation reports are to be shared with the supervisor.

At the end of the second semester the supervisor is asked to provide a brief evaluation report to the student and to the Field Education staff. The format of this report will be suggested in a form provided by the Field Education office. This is to be shared with the student prior to submission to the Field Education office. It will be kept on file in the Field Education office and, in the case of CSC Seminarians, in the office of the Superior of Moreau Seminary.

The Directors of the Notre Dame Field Education Program will provide a series of Supervisors' Sessions at regular intervals over the academic year. These sessions serve as opportunities for ongoing discussion and review of the essential elements of supervision in ministry.

Supervision of Field Education Students

Supervision is a vital component of field education for ministry. Regular critical reflection on experience enables students to integrate theory, practice, self understanding and skills.

A skilled supervisor possesses not only good listening skills but also the ability to raise critical questions. The supervisor provides a supportive relationship while maintaining professional distance, is open to a variety of viewpoints, and encourages creativity and independent thinking.

It is the role of the supervisor:

(1) To provide a brief description of the field setting and a general job description of the student's work. The student will write a specific job description.

(2) To assist the student in developing an appropriate contract.

(3) To meet with the student once a week for a supervisory session. It is the student's responsibility to set the agenda for this meeting. This is usually done through a journal which is presented to the supervisor 24 hours in advance of the meeting.

(4) To provide a written evaluation of the student twice a year. At midyear this involves filling out a short form. At the end of the year a longer written evaluation is requested.

(5) To contact the Field Education Director (239-6493) in the unlikely event that a problem should arise.

Supervisor Guidelines

Because we believe that supervision is a vital component of the Field Education experience, we have drawn up the following guidelines:

(1) We expect the supervisor to have had at least three years of full-time ministerial experience.

(2) We expect the supervisor to have worked at the site for at least one year prior to becoming a supervisor for that site.

(3) Persons considering the role of supervisor in our program for the first time are expected to comply with the following:

(a) an interview with the director of Field Education,

(b) submission of a brief curriculum vitae,

(c) attendance at an orientation meeting in September or October.

(4) All supervisors are expected to attend the autumn workshop. If this workshop is missed for two consecutive years the supervisor may be asked to withdraw from the Field Education program.

(5) Supervisors assume the following responsibilities regarding the students:

(a) assist students in drawing up their contract,

(b) meet weekly for 1/2 hour for supervision, using the student's journal or other written matter as agenda,

(c) evaluate at year's end the student's participation in ministry,

(d) contact the director of Field Education in case of serious dereliction of duty.

Styles of Supervision

Task Oriented:

    Primary Goal—accomplish certain tasks
    Focus of Attention—evaluation of performance of tasks
    Supervisor's Task—define work responsibilities; see work is done
    Student's Task—give account of how one is acquiring the knowledge and skills in performing the assigned tasks
    Influences in Relationship—supervisor has the responsibility for seeing tasks are accomplished; student is seen as a member of the staff or as a colleague

Apprentice:

    Primary Goal—student socialized to profession by sharing in work of supervisor
    Focus of Attention—what, why, and how supervisor does what is done
    Supervisor's Task—involve the student in one's work
    Student's Task—shares in the same duties as supervisor; learning takes place through observing and modeling
    Influences in Relationship—supervisor shares his/her work with the student; student may eventually be given separate responsibilities

Training:

    Primary Goal—socialization of student into a profession and role
    Focus of Attention—personal and professional growth of the student
    Supervisor's Task—design a learning context and establish a contract
    Student's Task—to speak of one's personal and professional questions arising from ministerial situations requires student to articulate expectations of desired learning
    Influences in Relationship—supervisor determines professional activities of student; provides exposure to models for professional identity

Resource:

    Primary Goal—develop student's awareness and utilization of resources
    Focus of Attention—determine what resources the student needs for effective project

Supervisor's Task—assist the student to reflect on the project to determine resources needed

Student's Task—to assess and reflect on the operation of the project and articulate to the supervisor information and assistance needed

Influences in Relationship—joint discussion of ways to approach a situation and resources needed to carry out project; a sense of collegiality often prevails

Consultative:

Primary Goal—expand student's ability to clarify issues and goals, and problem solve

Focus of Attention—deal with issues, goals, and problems of concern to the student

Supervisor's Task—establish a consulting contract with the student and know the skills of consultation

Student's Task—to articulate one's point of view; the ultimate responsibility for solving problems rests with the student

Influences in Relationship—student has the larger responsibility for defining the context

Supervisor Profile

Field Setting _____

Address _____

Name_____Office Tel #_____

Position held in setting _____

Education: (Complete all lines applicable)

College_____Degree_____

Seminary_____Degree_____

Graduate_____Degree_____

Other (special training or course work)

_____

_____

Professional/Vocational Experience

(list positions held)

_____

_____

_____

Please list any training experiences you may have had in supervision:

Please list past supervisory experiences:

Signature _____

Mid-Year Report: Supervisor

Student_____

Supervisor_____ Site_____

Please check the appropriate column regarding your evaluation of this student.
VG = Very Good   G = Good   F = Fair
VG   G   F

Personal work habits

Punctuality
Keeping appointments
Handles absences responsibly
Preparation for assignments

Relation to church or agency

Meets agency obligations
Understands agency goals and objectives
Follows proper channels in functioning

Relationships with people

Works comfortably with staff
Relates well to others
Assumes responsibility for his or her part in relationships

Functioning within expected role

Exercises initiative in fulfilling assignments
Protects confidentiality
Understands role as helping (enabling) individuals
Is creative in completion of tasks
Is a good leader

Supervisory relationship

Assumes responsibility for participation in conference
Submits records when required
Handles criticism well
Evaluates supervisor's suggestions before acting upon them

How often have you met with student?

Field Education Mid-Year Report (Student)

I. Regarding Your Goals: Please read your contract. Does each of your goals, as stated in your learning contract, continue to be appropriate to your work and your own intentions? If so, why? If not, restate any goal which is no longer appropriate.

II. Regarding Supervision:
1. How often have you met with your supervisor?
2. How long were the meetings?
3. How have you used your journal for supervision?
4. In what ways has supervision been helpful? How might it be improved?

III. Supervisor's Response: Is there any issue that your supervisor finds appropriate to raise at this juncture?

End of Year Report (Supervisor)

Memo to: Field Education Supervisors
    From: Regina Coll, C.S.J.
            Director of Field Education
    Subj: Supervisor's Summary Report

1. Please write a summary report of the Master of Divinity student who has been working with you this past year. Include some of the following issues:
    a. Learning goals the student has been working on
    b. Strengths evident in the student's work
    c. Skills which need improvement
2. Please describe how supervision was carried out and how helpful, in your judgment, the supervisory sessions were to the student.
3. Please add any other remarks you may wish.

Field Education End of Year Report (Student)
Master of Divinity Program
University of Notre Dame

Name: _____

Site: _____

Supervisor: _____

Please use these questions as guidelines. Write your report on a separate paper, affix signatures to that paper, and attach it to this form.

1. Indicate a significant issue that has surfaced in your field work. Describe how you addressed it, and what you learned from it.

2. What have you learned about your pastoral identity?
   a. What are some of your natural strengths?
   b. What skills have you developed this year?
   c. What limitations have you discovered in yourself?
   d. What skills would you like to focus on for further development?

3. In your supervisory meetings, which tools did you find most helpful? In what ways were they helpful?
   a. learning contract
   b. personal journal
   c. field education journal
   d. other

4. In what ways have your supervisory meetings been helpful?

5. Please invite your supervisor to add comments or observations if that is desirable.

Recommendation for Ministry

The students in the University of Notre Dame Master of Divinity Program are preparing for ministry in the Roman Catholic Tradition. The University of Notre Dame is a certifying agency for the Congregation of Holy Cross and for prospective employers regarding the fitness of each student for ministry. As supervisors, you share in that responsibility.

We ask you to consider seriously the requirements for public ministry, some of which are listed on the accompanying evaluation form. In the light of these and other considerations which you may wish to add, we ask:

Do you recommend the student_____
for ministry within the Roman Catholic Tradition?

Indicate the degree of recommendation:

_____Strongly recommend

_____Recommend

_____Recommend with reservation

_____Do not recommend

Signature _____

Date_____

Index